The
Husband's
Toolbox

by

Pastor Steve Morgan

www.ForHimMinistries.net

TABLE OF CONTENTS

TABLE OF CONTENTS .... *III*

FORWARD .... *V*

ACKNOWLEDGMENTS .... *VII*

MY TESTIMONY .... *IX*

A MEDIATOR .... *- 1 -*

THE RIGHT BLUEPRINT .... *- 6 -*

FORGIVENESS .... *- 13 -*

THE NATURE OF THINGS .... *- 21 -*

TRUE LOVE .... *- 35 -*

THE RELATOR & THE WARRIOR .... *- 40 -*

STOP SHOUTING! I CAN'T HEAR YOU. .... *- 44 -*

WHAT DOES A WOMAN NEED? .... *- 46 -*

TAKE THE CHALLENGE! .... *- 60 -*

YOUR ROLE .... *- 68 -*

THE TOOL BOX .... *- 73 -*

    TRUST IS EARNED! .... - 76 -

    DICTIONARIES .... - 78 -

    I NEED.... I NEED .... - 80 -

    CUSTOMER SERVICE .... - 82 -

    DON'T ASSUME YOU KNOW? .... - 84 -

    DECISIONS.. - 86 -

    GIVE WHAT YOU'RE GIVEN... - 92 -

    ARTIFICIAL INTUITION (AI) .... - 94 -

    CHANGING CHANNELS .... - 95 -

    TYPES OF AUTHORITY .... - 97 -

    MENOPAUSE.. - 99 -

    TIMING IS EVERYTHING! .... - 102 -

    BOUNDARIES; YOUR PROTECTION! .... - 104 -

    HAVING FUN! .... - 108 -

TABLE OF CONTENTS
(Continued)

WHAT ABOUT THE CHILDREN? .... *- 111 -*

IRON SHARPENS IRON .... *- 114 -*

TAKE ACTION .... *- 117 -*

FORWARD

Men, God never intended for you to be frustrated in your marriage. He wants you to be the leading entity He designed for you to be. In this book, you will learn of your tools for marriage and how to use them God's way. Rest assured, you and your marriage will never be the same.

Marriage really isn't hard. We make it hard because of our misconceptions and the way we go about doing things. But God made it easy as we look into the bible for His answers.

I made it hard on myself because I didn't know what the bible says about this lifestyle. That is why I wrote this book; to help others avoid some of the frustration I went through.

If you want to know what Marriage is all about, and how to make it work, this book is for you. I will be explaining from a biblical perspective how God designed the man and woman and their unique capabilities. These principles are core abilities given by God and I have proven them to be true in Africa, Honduras, Jamaica and all over the USA.

If you are a new groom, this book will help you avoid some of the landmines that others have faced.

After reading this book, you will know how to dynamically change the meaning of marriage into heaven on earth. All this, while having fun too.

ACKNOWLEDGMENTS

I have eternal gratitude to my Lord Jesus Christ who is my all in all. To my wife, Georgette, who has always supported me in my endeavors; you are my queen. To my daughter Kiliea and son Michael Jr., whom I love very much; my greatest gift to you is what the Lord Jesus Christ has taught me.

There have been some significant men and women of God in my life. This book is possible because of their love, demonstration of Godliness and scriptural knowledge. We all are a summation of our exposures. I am blessed to be exposed to all mentioned here and my encounters with them.
:

- Apostle B. R. Hicks ~ Christ Gospel International, Jeffersonville, Indiana. A mighty woman of God who poured a deep foundation in my life. Thank you for your Labor of Love.

- Bishop Anthony and Pastor Kelly McMillan ~ Pensacola Life Church, Pensacola, Florida. Thank you for your support, encouragement and love; you have become a pillar in my life.

- Apostle Nate and Pastor Valerie Holcomb ~ Christian House of Prayer, Killeen, Texas. Thank you for your ministry, insight, wisdom, understanding and patience.

- Pastor Chris and Nikki Mathis ~ The Summit Church, Crestview, Florida. You have been the Balm of

Gilead for my wife and I after a rough work. Thank you for showing us what it looks like to be a Christian and Pastor.

- Pastor Philip Campbell ~ Abundant Life Ministries. You are an anointed leader in the body of Christ and have always been one who reminds me of the need to stay in the spirit of God.

A special thanks to all the couples who allowed me to use them in my study cases. Your transparency has made you real instruments to helping others succeed in their marriage.

Thanks to all who allowed me to use them as a sounding board for clarity while writing this book.

To my sister Candis, who helped me create the book cover... When we were kids, we played a game...Cha Ching Ching!

MY TESTIMONY

My parents were not avid church goers. In fact, the main moral guidance given as I was a teenager was that I would be in serious trouble if I got anyone pregnant.

I saw my mom and dad argue many times. I never saw them sit down and discuss things or resolve problems calmly. My exposure was not of the best way to handle things. It was my salvation with Jesus Christ that embarked me on a journey to development in all aspects of my life to include dealing with conflict in the relationship. Not that I'm perfect by any stretch of the imagination, but I strive to master these principles every day.

Much of my knowledge of marriage comes from the bible, some pastors and being married since 1984 with my wife. I have learned much from her and still do.

I once built a 1000 square foot steel metal building by myself and I sought God on how to accomplish many tasks. I needed the right tools to do the job and this book is an attempt to pass on to you the right tools that I am perfecting concerning marriage.

In my marriage, I was confronted with a difficult task of being the husband to my wife and I sought God for the answers. It wasn't long before I was asking: "What does my wife want from me?". The end result was "The Husband's Toolbox." As a man, I need some tools to work with to succeed with my wife. In what appears to be a moving target, I have found some core needs she has that I can count on to be the husband that she needs.

Through prayer and studying the word of God, I found some core needs that every woman has that I think will help you tremendously. These core needs are universal and I have proven them in several continents. I then sought to find out what role does the man play in meeting those needs. It is in this research that I have written the Husband's Toolbox. I was surprised to find how powerful and influential these core needs are when met. In fact, a woman can know what her husband is doing and still not resist him.

Pray with me:

Lord, cover me with your blood. Forgive me of my sins; known and unknown according to your word. Open my eyes of understanding. Let me see your word from your perspective and not mine. In Jesus' name, I pray, Amen.

1

A MEDIATOR

When a man and a woman marry, the picture is incomplete. An impartial mediator is necessary to help each person to make adjustments that will promote a perfect union. This mediator must be one of authority; one who you revere greater than all things. The best authority is the creator of marriage; God. God's son, Jesus Christ and His directions on marriage gives us a 100% chance for success.

As a person who strives to follow the word of God, I try to disregard how I feel. I find that when I obey the word, things turn out so much better. If I go by my feelings, I just make things worse for myself and others. Following the word of God and the leading of the Holy Ghost is the best way to change a marriage from good to better.

The information in this book is predicated that you have a personal relationship with Jesus Christ. In order to get the results you are looking for, you will need to know Jesus Christ as your Savior AND Lord. So, let's start from the beginning.

SALVATION

Has anyone ever told you that God loves you and that He has a wonderful plan for your life?

I have a quick, but important question to ask you. God forbid, but if you were to die this second, do you know for sure, beyond a shadow of a doubt, that you would go to Heaven?

Let me quickly share with you what the Holy Bible relays. It reads "**for all have sinned and come short of the glory of God (Romans 3:23)**" and "**for the wages of sin is death, but the gift of God is eternal life through Jesus Christ our Lord (Romans 6:23)**". The Bible also reads, "**For whosoever shall call upon the name of the Lord shall be saved (Romans 10:13)**". Would you say that you and I are a "whosoever"? Of course, we are; all of us are.

If you would like to receive the gift God has for you today, say this prayer with your heart and voice out loud.

Dear Lord Jesus, come into my heart, forgive me of my sin. Wash me and cleanse me. Set me Free. Jesus, I thank You that You died for me. I believe that You are the son of God, you died on the cross for my sins and that you rose from the dead to set me free. Fill me with the Holy Ghost. Give me a passion for the lost, a hunger for the things of God, and a holy boldness, to preach the gospel of Jesus Christ. In Jesus' name, I pray, Amen.

Now you can say "I'm Saved: I'm born again, I'm forgiven, and I'm on my way to Heaven, because I have Jesus in my heart!"

As a minister of the gospel of Jesus Christ, I tell you today that all of your sins are forgiven. Always remember to run to God and not from Him because He loves you and has a great plan for your life.

Welcome to the family of God!

Now you have a mediator who will comfort, protect and stick up for you while correcting you. The chances of your marriage being a success have just increased by 100-fold. Congratulations! Your mediator never sleeps and is always there for you. You just call out to Jesus and He will hear you. He will also answer if you just listen with your spirit man.

I can honestly say that Jesus is the mediator that gets all the credit; my wife and I have been married since June 1984. There have been several times when Jesus instructed me to humble myself, and through obedience, He worked it out. You just can't go wrong with an all knowing, all seeing God as your mediator.

To ensure you have a good foundation, I encourage you to read my other books as well:

First Things First (What Every Christian Should Know)

Second Things Second (The Doctrine of Christ)

Now let's look at some principles for your marriage. Like all principles, if you work with them, they will help you and if you violate them, they will hurt you.

YOUR MEDIATOR

Now that you have Jesus as your mediator, he will speak on how you should conduct yourself. He will tell you in the moment what to say, what not to say, what to do and what not to do. He's the one that will tell you to apologize and ask for forgiveness.

Not everything Jesus tells you to do will be easy but, if you deny yourself the right to do or say what you want, you will see your desires come to pass. This is because we are our greatest enemy when it comes to success. This applies to marriage, friendship, business and all other facets of our lives.

In my earlier years of marriage, my wife and I would be at a standoff after an argument. She would not budge nor would I. I remember thinking "I am NOT going to apologize!" Then a small still voice in my heart would reach all the way to my head and say "Yes you are." I knew that it was God on many levels but the first level is: The enemy of marriage will never tell you to apologize; he revels in stubbornness and pride. I had to humble myself and obey God's voice and apologize.

The more I obeyed His voice, the more He spoke to me. I realized that being led by the Holy Ghost is not an accident. It is a purposeful intention to resist all other influences that contradict what He is telling me. These influences are my thoughts and reasoning, my feelings (emotional needs), desires, bodily needs, other people's opinions, society's culture and finally the "everybody is doing it" dogma.

Your mediator wants you to succeed in all facets of your life; to include your marriage. So, His motivation is to see you win! That is why you can trust Him. Jesus is an all knowing, all powerful, omni-present God who will use all to tell you what to do; the outcome will be better than you can imagine. Don't be afraid to be obedient rather leap confidently into your heavenly father's arms. Picture yourself like a child who jumps off the bed into their parent's arms; He will catch you. At first you may need to force yourself to do the right thing and as you are obedient, you will experience a freedom that comes only through doing or saying what is right. The more you practice obedience the more liberty and freedom you will experience. Soon you will run to the obedience corner knowing that your LIFE and LIBERTY comes only from your obedience.

This principle of obedience pertains to every aspect of your life. Jesus wants to liberate your thoughts and give you peace that passes all understanding. He wants to teach you how to speak life and not death to your life as well as others. Jesus will show you how do things that promote peace with yourself and others around you. He is Very interested in what we think, say and do. After all, you are a representative of Him now. You are an ambassador for Jesus Christ on this earth and a witness to heaven of His great love.

2

THE RIGHT BLUEPRINT

Male or female, we all want the perfect relationship where both partners are fulfilled. It's just that we don't really know how to go about getting it. It's not like we are given a book of instructions on how to assemble this complicated mechanism we call marriage. Or are we?

WHAT BLUEPRINT ARE YOU USING?

When building a house, ONE blueprint is used to ensure that all the plumbing, electrical, air conditioning, rooms and closets work together in a cohesive manner. If more than one blueprint is used, the whole project is destined to fail.

There are two blueprints used in today's society for marriage: the worldly blueprint, and the Godly blueprint. These two blueprints, if mixed, will produce failure. The worldly blueprint was designed by Lucifer (the enemy) to produce failure in marriage.

The Godly blueprint has the power to transform the worst marriage into heaven on earth. Practicing principles out of the Word of God (Bible) will fulfill both the husband and wife. God is flawless, His instructions cannot fail. Like my grandmother-in-law used to sing "Well I know my Bible is right! Somebody else is wrong."

Our goal in this life is to diligently work on perfecting our ability to apply the Godly blueprint. This is a developmental process; not a quick work. So be patient with yourself and your spouse.

Your best effort is to get back up and try again when you have failed. According to Proverbs, you are considered a just person if you get up and try again. This is important to know: we can begin again when we make mistakes!

Pr 24:16 For a just man falleth seven times, and riseth up again: but the wicked shall fall into mischief.

Notice here that the wicked don't try to stand up. I want to encourage you to keep applying these principles no matter how many times you think you have gotten it wrong; just stand back up and try again. The art of learning is repetition.

Determine today that you are going to use the bible (God's Word) to be your blueprint for how you will conduct yourself with your loved ones from now on. You will find it so much easier. This is Jesus' plan from the beginning! Jesus said in Matthew 11:

Mt 11:28 Come unto me, all [ye] that labour and are heavy laden, and I will give you rest. **29** Take my yoke upon you, and learn of me; for I am meek and lowly in heart: and ye shall find rest unto your souls. **30** For my yoke [is] easy, and my burden is light.

You really can find rest in your marriage by using the bible as your blueprint for marriage.

IF I WERE THE ENEMY!

Marriage is symbolic of Jesus the Groom and His Bride. If I were the enemy, I would try to destroy every resemblance of Jesus and His marriage. Even more importantly, to destroy a marriage that claims Jesus Christ as their Lord would prove that God's word does not work and that He is a liar. Disproving the word of God has been Lucifer's biggest marketing strategy. Satan loves to see people fail in marriage, especially those who profess to have Jesus Christ in their heart.

One of the tricks the enemy uses, is to train up men and women to adopt his failed problem solving skills. It starts by exposing you to the actions of others (your parents or other adults) while you are young to lead you to believe it is acceptable behavior. Naturally, you may repeat what you've seen because this may be all you know. So, the failed technique propagates to the next generation. The enemy does this just to spread worldwide failure in relationships. This is his nature. Jesus described him perfectly in John 10.

Joh 10:10 The thief cometh not, but for to steal, and to kill, and to destroy: I am come that they might have life, and that they might have [it] more abundantly.

The enemy wants to kill all of our dreams, steal all hope away from us and destroy everything that is good in our lives. BUT GOD provides a better solution! I love that Jesus finishes His statement with an opposing solution to the enemy's plan. Abundant Life!

Now that you know that the enemy wants to destroy your marriage and you are aware of his intentions, it should be easier for you to choose the correct blueprint from the designer of marriage; God. He designed marriage to succeed. Actually, I have yet to meet anyone who gets married just to get a divorce.

THE OWNER'S MANUAL

When I take my car to the shop, I try to take it to the manufacturer so that it can be repaired correctly. Most manufacturers that offer customer service train their technicians on the systems that they will be servicing. It may be a little more expensive at the front end, but for the most part, I have saved time and money for not having to deal with rework issues.

In order for me to use an owner's manual of a specific car, I must first own the product that I have the manual for. This is true with the Bible also. Salvation is like possessing the product and once you have it, all the warranties and rights of the owner's manual are legally yours. The Bible is your manual, and if applied and followed properly, it can help you immensely.

If you are going to use the bible as the blueprint for your relationships, then it would be most effective if you received salvation. To do that, go to the first chapter entitled A Mediator and it will lead you through a prayer for salvation.

Once you have prayed and asked Jesus into your heart, you can say "I'm the rightful owner of all warrantees and guarantees, because I have Jesus in my heart!"

Remember! You can stand on this because it says so in the bible. It's not based on how you feel or think about it. It's based on God's pre-established blueprint or owner's manual. The bible says in Romans 10:

Ro 10:9 That if thou shalt confess with thy mouth the Lord Jesus, and shalt believe in thine heart that God hath raised him from the dead, thou shalt be saved. **10** For with the heart man believeth unto righteousness; and with the mouth confession is made unto salvation. **11** For the scripture saith, Whosoever believeth on him shall not be ashamed. **12 ¶** For there is no difference between the Jew and the Greek: for the same Lord over all is rich unto all that call upon him. **13** For whosoever shall call upon the name of the Lord shall be saved.

As a minister of the gospel of Jesus Christ, I tell you today that all of your sins are forgiven. Always remember to **run to God** and not from Him because He loves you and has a great plan for your life.

Welcome to the family of God!

God has made it clear what constitutes salvation. Receiving salvation, entering into the kingdom of heaven, receiving Christ in your heart, and being born again are phrases that the Christian community uses to define joining the Family of God; they're synonymous.

God's word is the measuring stick by which we will be judged on the Day of Judgment so read the bible on a daily basis; even if it is just one line.

I recommend starting with the New Testament first because it is Jesus Christ revealed; the Old Testament is Jesus Christ concealed; many hidden revelations of Him. It's easier to see Jesus in the Old Testament once you are familiar with Him in the New Testament. Also, don't worry about what you don't understand in the bible, if you just work with what you do understand, you will be busy enough. The bible is a living document and the Holy Ghost will make clear to you what you need to understand at that moment.

Prayer: Speak to God daily. Start with Hello Jesus. If you speak to him like you do your best friend, you get so much further in your relationship. Of course, if you must make it difficult, you can put marbles in your mouth and try to speak in the old language. Say something like:

> Lordeth Godeth, I praiseth thee for the wonderfulleth things that thou hast doneth for me. Blesseth me this dayeth Lordeth! Ameneth!! [I'm kidding about this prayer and the marbles]

It is good to thank Jesus for all that He has done and is doing in your life on a regular basis. It's a great prayer.

I always start off with this:

> Lord Jesus, forgive me of my sins that I have committed known and unknown against your word. Thank you for your many blessings that you have given me.

I ask that you …

Take care of ….

Help me to …

Move on my family's behalf.

Bless my Pastor…

Bless my enemies to know you more.

In Jesus Name I pray, Amen.

It is prayer that will help you complete the challenges in this book. I know you will succeed!

Jesus taught us to pray in Matthew 6: 9-15

Mt 6:9 ¶ After this manner therefore pray ye: Our Father which art in heaven, Hallowed be thy name.**10** Thy kingdom come. Thy will be done in earth, as [it is] in heaven. **11** Give us this day our daily bread. **12** And forgive us our debts, as we forgive our debtors. **13** And lead us not into temptation, but deliver us from evil: For thine is the kingdom, and the power, and the glory, for ever. Amen. **14** For if ye forgive men their trespasses, your heavenly Father will also forgive you: **15** But if ye forgive not men their trespasses, neither will your Father forgive your trespasses.

3

FORGIVENESS

I find that there is a greater issue that prevents men from living in their God ordained position in the marriage. Taking the challenges in this book opens the door for a dramatic change towards your success in your relationship.

Like all great achievements, there are barriers that must be overcome to reach the final goal. When it comes to relationships, a huge barrier is un-forgiveness. I have seen more people induce sickness, cancer and many other ailments to include unhappiness, depression and finally suicide; all because of unforgiveness. God never designed the human body to shoulder the weight of un-forgiveness.

Most men find it very difficult to have compassion for their spouse when they are angry or harboring resentment towards their wives or others. The sad part is they are only hurting themselves more.

The enemy doesn't want you to press into forgiveness. He knows that if you do, he will lose his persuasive power that he has over you. Please remember that Lucifer, Satan, the

Devil, intends to destroy you for now and forever. Telling you that you can forgive but not forget is one of his greatest tricks. Just let it go.

MY TESTAMONY

When I first received Jesus into my heart, I was struggling with getting high. My guilt and condemnation was so much that every sermon I heard seemed to speak against it. I prayed and sought Jesus to help me quit for weeks, when He finally led me to my need to forgive my father. I wanted nothing to do with this subject but I could no longer ignore it. It took me about three months to get my head and heart right to call my father. I told him that I forgave him for the things that he did to me. He replied "I don't know what you are talking about." The next Sunday after church I sat in the same car, in the same seat with the same person that I got high with and when he offered it to me, I thought I was going to throw up! I couldn't do it! Since that time, I have never had a need or a desire to get high again. Praise the Lord!

One of the lessons I have learned here, is that our actions are a product of what is in our heart. The cause is located in our heart. If I fix the cause, the effect will go away. My un-forgiveness of my father was keeping me bound to other sins. Once I forgave my father, regardless of his response, I was set free from an entanglement that I couldn't shake on my own.

This is not about the other person! It's about you getting set free from a very destructive force. Once set free, you can relate with your wife without the influence of un-forgiveness tainting your messages.

THE BENEFITS OF FORGIVENESS

Staying in the state of forgiveness reaps many benefits. It protects us from the spirit of bondage. Forgiveness empowers us to keep His peace. We experience a new sense of hope and joy and are able to live our lives guilt free. The effects that have been difficult to get control of due to un-forgiveness no longer have any strength. Your joy returns, hope and strength is regained and you are free!

GOD'S EXAMPLE

God's plan concerning forgiveness is very clear from Jesus' example and his instructions. Let's take a look at what the bible says.

Mt 18:21 ¶ Then came Peter to him, and said, Lord, how oft shall my brother sin against me, and I forgive him? till seven times? **22** Jesus saith unto him, I say not unto thee, Until seven times: but, Until seventy times seven.

Jesus didn't make this stance to be difficult or challenging. He knew what un-forgiveness does to us and wanted to show us a way out.

If you are a human being, then you have been and/or will be hurt. Some of these incidents may have been imposed upon you with no fault of your own. A trust that was betrayed, verbal abuse, physical abuse, molestation, rape and many other forms of offense can affect us to our core being. Regardless of what we have experienced, it is within our power to choose to forgive. Forgiveness is the first step to complete healing in your body, soul and spirit.

Mt 6:14 For if ye forgive men their trespasses, your heavenly Father will also forgive you: **15** But if ye forgive not men their trespasses, neither will your Father forgive your trespasses.

Even the Lord 's Prayer includes "Forgive us our trespasses as we forgive those who trespass against us".

You should now understand why I say that you must forgive ALL who have hurt you. It is for your benefit that you forgive.

YOU MUST DECIDE TO FORGIVE FOR YOUR SAKE!

Forgiveness is not an emotion; it is a deliberate act on your part; a decision. If forgiveness is a feeling, then I wonder what Jesus felt when he was beaten and hung on the cross. In fact, while hanging on the cross, in the middle of his gasps for air, he said:

Lu 23:34 Then said Jesus, Father, forgive them; for they know not what they do. And they parted his raiment, and cast lots.

One of the questions I ask myself before I justify holding a grudge is "Have I been treated worse than the crucifixion of my Lord Jesus?" My answer is always "NO". Therefore, I am obligated to forgive.

FORGET ABOUT IT

To what degree are we to forgive? Let's look at God's example of forgiveness:

Jer 31:34 And they shall teach no more every man his neighbour, and every man his brother, saying, Know the LORD: for they shall all know me, from the least of them unto the greatest of them, saith the LORD: for **I will forgive their iniquity, and I will remember their sin no more.**

Forgetting about something done to you is not suggesting that we practice selective amnesia, it is the practice of not allowing your memories to persuade you to do anything contrary to the word of God. For example:

Jas 4:17 Therefore to him that knoweth to do good, and doeth [it] not, to him it is sin.

Notice that this is not predicated on whether someone hurt you.

THE PROCESS OF FORGIVING

In order for you to start the process of forgiveness, you must begin by speaking it with your voice. Read aloud the prayer that Jesus said to pray:

Matthew 6:10 After this manner therefore pray ye: Our Father which art in heaven, Hallowed be thy name. **10** Thy kingdom come. Thy will be done in earth, as it is in heaven. **11** Give us this day our daily bread. **12** And forgive us our debts, as we forgive our debtors. **13** And lead us not into temptation, but deliver us from evil: For thine is the kingdom, and the power, and the glory, forever. Amen. **14** For if ye forgive men their trespasses, your heavenly Father will also forgive you: **15** But if ye forgive not men their trespasses, neither will your Father forgive your trespasses.

Right now! I want you to say "I forgive (the person that hurt you) and I forgive myself". If you find it difficult to say it for the first time then you are definitely working on the right issue. Once you have said it once, you must say it several times more and then every day until there is no emotional connection left.

Once you start the process of forgiveness, your Father in heaven forgives you. The bondage of un-forgiveness will fall off of you like autumn leaves. You will begin to experience the joy and freedom you were intended to live.

With this barrier removed, you now have the Grace to continue with these challenges and reap the benefits. You are more than a conqueror... So, start changing your destiny!

Notice that Jesus directs us to pray "Thy will be done in earth, as it is in heaven"? It is His intention to start heaven in you right now. This is how heaven comes to earth. He does it by bringing heaven in your life right now.

I know that some of the subjects in this book are difficult. But if you hang in there, I guarantee that Jesus will move on your behalf and perform miracles beyond your expectations.

Eph 3:20 Now unto him that is able to do exceeding abundantly above all that we ask or think, according to the power that worketh in us,

Let Jesus be the power that works in you and through you!

Forgiveness is a powerful weapon against the snares of the enemy. Do not under estimate how the enemy will try to influence you to keep an issue with someone. You will hear all sorts of justifications, in your thoughts and from others, to hold a grudge. God could have done the same to us; instead He died on the Cross. It didn't feel good but it was necessary. Forgiving may be difficult, but it is necessary.

It is my experience that forgiving others is not for them but for me. Doctors have confirmed that biologically, it is unhealthy to harbor ill will against someone. When I forgive someone, I release the pressures off of my life. I am willing to believe that Jesus has our joy in mind when he stresses the need to forgive.

I am reminded of a woman who the Holy Ghost revealed to me that she was harboring un-forgiveness against a man who physically abused her. As I prayed for her, the Lord led me to insist that she speak out that she forgives him. She struggled and strained to frame the words and finally she said them. It was clear that these were the hardest words that she had ever had to speak. Once she succeeded, a spirit of relief came over her and she wept in ecstasy as the Holy Ghost began to pour into her and minister to her needs. She was truly set free that day!

God is very interested in our ability to get along with others. To the point that Jesus gave these instructions:

Matt 5:23 Therefore if thou bring thy gift to the altar, and there rememberest that thy brother hath ought against thee; **24** Leave there thy gift before the altar, and go thy way; first be reconciled to thy brother, and then come and offer thy gift.

Let's be diligent at keeping un-forgiveness out of our heart!

When we forgive, we win and the testimony of Christ wins! Let's stay in the WIN – WIN business!

You must then bless the one you are forgiving. Jesus said:

Mt 5:44 But I say unto you, Love your enemies, bless them that curse you, do good to them that hate you, and pray for them which despitefully use you, and persecute you;

Your success in getting free of the bondage of un-forgiveness is hinged on whether you learn to forgive AND pray for those who have offended you.

Whatever wrong that has been done to you from whomever, past or present, you must choose to forgive. It is your only way out of the bondage.

HOW DO I FORGIVE?

1. Choose to forgive
2. Speak out your forgiveness aloud often
3. Bless the one you are forgiving in prayer

Here is an example prayer:

Lord Jesus, forgive me of all my sins, known and unknown according to your word. Help me to stay in forgiveness as you forgive me. I forgive (name). Now I bless (name) and pray that you touch them and move on their behalf for your cause.

YOU CAN DO THIS!!!

Php 4:13 I can do all things through Christ which strengtheneth me.

4

THE NATURE OF
THINGS

Now that we are using the bible to determine how we operate in our marriage, let's look at some revelatory information about men and women.

Through some study, I have found that the Hebrew word for Name can be translated as Nature. So when we examine the Hebrew definition of a name, we are looking into the nature of that being. So let's look at some Hebrew definitions.

When we look up the Hebrew definition for the words Man, Dominion, Created, Male and Female, we see a unique picture into the order of Gods Plan.

Gen 1:26 ¶ And God said, Let us make **man** in our image, after our likeness: and let them have **dominion** over the fish of the sea, and over the fowl of the air, and over the cattle, and over all the earth, and over every creeping thing that creepeth upon the earth.

The Hebrew definition for **Man** is אדם adam (pronounced *aw-dawm'*) *m*eaning: Mankind

So, all of mankind was called Man and Man was to have Dominion over the earth. The Hebrew definition for **Dominion** follows:

Dominion - רדה radah (pronounced raw-daw')

1) Rule

2) Dominion

3) Take

4) Prevaileth

5) Reign

6) Ruler

7) Tread down

8) Subjugate

Mankind has been assigned to dominate the earth which was delegated by God. Please note that this is not divided among gender; rather given to all of Mankind.

Gen 1:27 So God **created** man in his own image, in the image of God created he him; **male** and **female** created he them.

Here we see that God in his infinite wisdom and balance created a balanced creature called Mankind. Mankind was **created** which means:

Hebrew - Meaning:

Created - ברא bara' (pronounced baw-raw')

    1) Shaped, Formed or Fashioned

    2) To be Chosen

    3) Dispatched

    4) Made Fat

So when God created mankind, he shaped him in balance as a combination of male and female. This is before the female was drawn from the rib. Here is a perfect picture of God in his perfect balance. As one, the male and female influence was destined to have dominion over all the earth; just as God has dominion over the heavens. God shaped, formed and fashioned us in His image, chose us, dispatched us and made us fat (or gave us the equipment) to do the assignment given. We have all that we need to succeed.

God has delegated His authority for dominance on the earth to Mankind. He does not interfere unless we request His intervention. You see, unlike some bosses we have worked for, who micro-manage your job, God will not micro-manage. This is why mankind must ask God for guidance and help, so that we can give God the liberty to work on the earth.

Now we know that the mission for Male and Female is the same, we can look at the differences to determine how each goes about accomplishing the same task.

MALE AND FEMALE

When God created mankind, he did not design them to hold or contain stress. He designed a relief mechanism that allows Mankind to vent stress successfully for better health. When God physically separated the male and female, the method of venting stress was split in two. Let's now look at how each deal with stress after the separation.

MALE

In Hebrew, the word "name" means nature. It should be no surprise that the Hebrew definition of **Male** is זכר zakawr meaning male gender of mankind. However, its root word sheds some light on the nature of the male:

> Root word to **Male** - זכר zakar (pronounced zaw-kar')
>
> 1) To Remember
> 2) Think
> 3) To mention

I would also like to add some additional traits here.

Warrior
Conqueror
Protector
Contemplator

This is not to say that the female does not remember things or that she does not think or mention things. This is simply to point out that males deal with stress differently. When a male is dealing with issues, he most likely is going to become "quieter" than usual. Men do not usually talk about issues to deal with stress. The male needs to process by thinking about the issue until he is relieved of the stress. Once he accomplishes this, he will most likely share with his spouse the issue. Mind you ladies, this could take days, weeks and even months. Be patient! Men get relief from stress when they can think it through. This is very therapeutic for us as our proclivity is to get relief by thinking about it. If a man is unable to think about an issue, he can't find relief from the pressure and will eventually seek means to get relief.

With this understanding, ladies, when your husband seems to be more distant, don't assume he is angry with you.

I would also like to point out some additional strengths of the Male; he is primarily visually stimulated. He is very keen to your touch as well. He is not verbally stimulated as much as the female.

FEMALE

As with the male, the Hebrew definition for **Female** is of no surprise:

> Meaning: נְקֵבָה neqebah (pronounced nek-ay-baw') meaning female, woman

> > The root word also sheds some light on the subject:

> Meaning: נָקַב naqab (pronounced naw-kab')

> > 1) Expressed

> > 2) Pierce Through

> > 3) Appoint

Additional study has shown that the female has additional strengths:

Nurturer

Nester

Relational

Like the male, the female was designed to deal with stress, but differently. When a female is stressed, she gets relief by expressing the issue. Her success in dealing with the stress is very high when she can express it to another person. Like men, once the stress has been dealt with, she can press on with other matters stress free. Women get relief from stress by discussing it.

When women have problems, they are more apt to talk about it. When they talk about it, they get the same relief as men do when they think about it. In fact, women don't need a solution most of the time; the act of expressing it actually sheds the pressure like taking off a raincoat.

I would like to point out that men think the same way women express it when it comes to dealing with stress; it's just that they don't verbalize it. If a man wrote down on a white board all the things he thinks when he is dealing with stress, and a woman wrote all the things she says on a white board, you would find that both sides look similar. This is why men must learn to wipe the board clean after listening to his wife; just as he does with his thoughts once relieved of stress.

One way ladies can help with this process is tell them what you need up front before you start de-stressing. This helps him know what is expected and he will gladly comply. If you need him to be a good listener, tell him. If you are looking for some advice, ask him for it and tell him that you want to explain the situation completely first.

One way to know if your man is confused on the role he needs to play is when you want him to be a listener and he starts giving you advice. Don't expect people to read your mind; tell them what you need.

One way husbands can stay on top of which role to play is if the wife forgets to inform them what is needed, he can simply ask: "Do you want my advice or are you in need of a good listener?"

Now that we know how each gender manages stress, let's be understanding of each other's processes and not force our methodology on each other. A typical comment from a woman to a man might be "why don't you just talk to me? You will feel better." She is unknowingly asking the man to change his nature to a female's. This only frustrates the male. On the other hand, the man might say, "why do you keep talking about the negative things? Can't you just let it go?" He is unknowingly asking her to be a man. This frustrates the woman.

I cannot stress this enough! It is very dangerous for a marriage to deny a specific nature to relieve itself from stress. The male should never ask the female to be a male (Don't express it until you have thought about it for a long while). Incidentally, if the man listens long enough, he will hear his wife give the solution that he was thinking. Likewise, the female should never ask the male to be a female (Talk to me!). Most men will talk about it once they get it figured out. Let's be patient enough to allow each other to process completely without the added pressure to do something against our nature.

LET'S MUDDY THE WATER

Now that I have given you the core functionality of the male and female, please be aware that there are various levels at which each operate. Some men will talk sooner than others and some women will refrain from talking more than others. This does not change what your core need is for stress relief. I'm only validating that there are more variables that will contribute to the level in which you operate. Some of these variables are: your temperament, your experiences, the culture you grew up in and several others.

Another factor to consider: the intensity of the stress will influence the amount of their core need to be satisfied. Some examples; an expresser may become quiet while mourning a lost love one. A contemplator may begin to chat over an upcoming event to relieve stress. Use this information loosely to allow your spouse to respond to dramatic moments in their own way. Patience is the most important tool here.

My advice to you is to apply the core fundamentals strictly speaking and allow your mate to vary it as they need. After some practice, you will learn the personal needs of your spouse.

YOU ARE THE ACCELEROMETER

In science, many instruments are used for quantifying measurements. There is a specific instrument we all have in common. It is the accelerometer.

The accelerometer does not sense consistency. It is only capable of sensing change. Aren't we just like that? We can ride in a car that keeps a steady direction and speed and we feel as if we are standing still. Just as soon as the car begins to turn or change speed, we sense the change. The stronger the change the more we are made aware of it. This is the purpose of this book. Men, I am asking you to take the challenges to expose your wife to some significant changes. Trust me when I say that you will get her undivided attention and drive her crazy with the need to understand where you are coming from. At the same time, you are going to have a blast.

THE POWER OF CHANGE IS FOR <u>YOUR</u> CHANGE

One of the biggest stumbling blocks in a relationship is when one person tries to change the other. Most of the time, the thing you are trying to change is an effect, not a cause. Only God knows why a person is doing something. He has to fix the cause in order for the change to be permanent.

HOWEVER! The only power we have is to change ourselves. You and God can work on the causes of your life to affect permanent change. You are responsible for accepting your spouse for who they are right now. You must work on changing you; not your spouse. It is in your change that will improve your relationship. When you change, in time, it will provoke a change in your spouse.

THE DANGER OF TESTS

I once was obsessing over who would do the dishes first. I would not do them to test my wife to see if she would do them. If she did not, then she failed my test and then I would become angry with her. These types of tests are unfair. We expect that our subject should know the rules of our test without our explanation. Before we justify our tests, let me ask you if you have ever been mentally or physically occupied that you did not notice the dishes or something else. EVERYONE has moments of being preoccupied to the point they are not as alert as other times. In the house especially, the home should be a place of safety to allow for such things. A home is a safe refuge from a demanding world. Why would we be so insensitive as to make the home anything less? Don't put people to the test. Give them rest!

LISTEN AT THE PITCH OF YOUR VOICE

One of the reasons the German language is considered very harsh is because they do not speak with intonation (change the pitch of their voice). It takes some effort for a German to learn English for this very reason. Learning the purpose of pitch can be a valuable tool to help you convey what you really mean.

When we greet someone, we instinctively raise the pitch of our voice; especially if we like them. Most of the time, the raised pitch is interpreted as excitement in seeing them and is considered a complement. We in turn would most likely raise our pitch without realizing it.

In most cases, the deeper the natural voice, the more one is likely to be misunderstood. I have a low pitch voice and it is naturally loud. My wife did not grow up around a lot of men and has occasionally perceived that I am upset when I am not. After several years of trying to figure out the cause of this misunderstanding, I realized that I would get a more positive result when I raised the tone of my voice just a bit. She then hears my message over the tone of my voice.

Try to practice changing the tone of your voice when you speak to someone and see the results you get. The balance to this is if you have a very high pitched voice, you might want to practice lowering the tone of you voice for better effect. I would recommend asking a friend for their opinion on your voice, and test the changes to see if you are getting the results that you desire. Besides, it might be fun to experiment with your friends.

HOW DO I DWELL WITH HER ACCORDING TO KNOWLEDGE?

1 Peter 3:7 Likewise, ye husbands, **dwell with them according to knowledge**, giving honour unto the wife, as unto the weaker vessel, and as being heirs together of the grace of life; that your prayers be not hindered.

What knowledge are you supposed to dwell with your wife? The simple answer is the knowledge she teaches you. I believe within her nature is the information you need to succeed in your relationship. However, you will not be able to receive it unless you lower your wall. The things she needs to share must enter your heart; not your head.

Lowering your wall allows what she is teaching you to enter your heart. Men, have a wall that acts like a reflex, it's important to learn how to resist and overcome your wall reflex so that you can dwell with your wife according to knowledge. Anything that is deposited into your head will be logically analyzed and sometimes dismissed; not that logic is a bad thing. It's just that you are dealing with her on a relational level; this level is higher than logic and can only be dealt with by the heart.

You may not be able to receive what she is trying to relay to you unless you learn how to keep your wall lowered. I will cover our wall that God has given us to perform with later.

Just know that if you keep causing your wife to stop talking to you, then you are not learning how to dwell with her with knowledge and you will fail.

My wife and I have had several conversations concerning my tone. Finally, I was able to share with her how I felt about this situation. I told her:

> A married couple will be more vulnerable to each other than other family and friends. This can make us more sensitive to each other. With that said, I need you to walk me through the times you hear a tone. I do not hear tones. If you cut our conversation off, then I will surely do it again because I don't get it.

> This is like the time my dad told me to wipe that look off my face and then he balled his fist and punched me in the face. I was nine years old and the only thing I felt was fear so I don't know what my face looked like... it sure wasn't defiance or disrespect. Maybe if he had said "Michael, I don't like it when you are frowning...it makes me think you are being disrespectful", then I would have known how to avoid getting punched the next time. Instead, I was vulnerable to his interpretation of something; to this day I have no idea what it is.

Do you like me being vulnerable to your interpretation with me having no idea? If not, then you must walk me through your definition of tones. When you hear one... use it as a teaching opportunity right then and there. This is the only way I know of how to fix this.

Much to my wife's credit, she agreed to try to teach me.

PRINCIPLE: Being right and delivering your point incorrectly is just as bad as being wrong.

You will get the same results as being wrong when you poorly deliver a right message.

Try starting off your conversations by telling your spouse your desired outcome. Maybe something like "I want us both to be satisfied with the outcome of our conversation. Here are my concerns..." And finally finish it off with "How do you see this and what ideas do you have for a compromise?" One of the biggest lessons I have learned is that my wife can be standing right next to me and still see something different.

It isn't always about who is right or wrong; sometimes it is about what makes you both happy.

SIDE NOTE: (Right and Wrong)

Please don't get caught up in the "who is right or who is wrong" mentality. This is a guarantee that you will never get past this obstacle. There is a higher order of thought that we must strive to achieve. It is the idea that being wrong is essential to discovering new truths about ourselves, our spouse, our children, our co-workers and our friends. It's an opportunity to learn some conditional facet that has never come up before. Being wrong isn't the only way to learn but it is just as essential as being right.

5

TRUE LOVE

When I think of true love, I think of Jesus Christ. He said in John 15:13:

John 15:13 Greater love hath no man than this, that a man lay down his life for his friends.

When we say that we love someone, do we mean that we will lay our lives down for that person? It is with this reckless abandonment of self that we find a force that knows no bounds; True Love.

You may have been taught that sex is Love, then you will need to study the true definition of True Love. I find 1Corinthians 13:1-7 to be an accurate account of perfect love. Notice that sex is not mentioned here.

1 Cor 13:1 Though I speak with the tongues of men and of angels, and have not love, I am become as sounding brass, or a tinkling cymbal. **2** And though I have the gift of prophecy, and understand all mysteries, and all knowledge; and though I have all faith, so that I could remove mountains, and have not love, I am nothing. **3** And though I bestow all my goods to feed the poor, and though I give my body to be burned, and have not love, it profiteth me nothing. **4** ¶ Love suffereth long, and is kind; love envieth not; love vaunteth not itself, is not puffed up, **5** Doth not behave itself unseemly, seeketh not her own, is not easily provoked, thinketh no evil; **6** Rejoiceth not in iniquity, but rejoiceth in the truth; **7** Beareth all things, believeth all things, hopeth all things, endureth all things. **8** ¶ Love never faileth: but whether there be prophecies, they shall fail; whether there be tongues, they shall cease; whether there be knowledge, it shall vanish away.

The word Love in John 15:13 and Charity in 1Corinthians 13:1 have the same meaning in the Greek. Which is αγαπη agape (pronounced ag-ah'-pay) meaning brotherly love.

When Jesus suffered many things, died and rose again to be with the Father in heaven, He introduced a new concept to the Greeks. Until then, there wasn't a word to describe the sacrificial love that Jesus gave for mankind. This is when the word Agape was created, which encapsulated a selfless disregard for the betterment of all others.

If you were to ask God why he loves you, He will not mention a physical attribute as a reason. God loves you because He does. Nothing you do or say will change His love for you. Think about it. If I say that I love you because you have a nice body, then when the body grows old, the love will also. My wife asked me why I loved her and I replied "I don't know. I just do". Later I learned this principle which made me feel great because I didn't need a reason to love her.

Please don't be hard on someone who gives a list of why they love you. They may feel pressured to qualify their love for you because of your question. They may not know this principle that love just loves for no reason at all. The best thing to do is tell them that you love them and that you can't explain it; you just don't know why.

LOVE IS NOT A FEELING! IT IS A COMMITMENT.

Love is a commitment! Emotional "warm fuzzies" come and go but a real commitment will endure sacrifice. This is why the scriptures state that God loves us so much that He gave His only begotten son (Jesus Christ) so that we could live. As a father, I don't think that I could give my son away. Yet, God did it for us. This is a painful sacrifice for any father. Jesus suffered many things to fulfill the punishment of sin. All because of his love for us. He knew that He was going to suffer and did not stray away from His commitment towards us. Jesus loves us so much that nothing could stop Him from fulfilling His commitment to suffer for us. Love is not a feeling…It is a commitment!

Love doesn't always feel good; it is not always convenient or easy. Love is a commitment. So, commit to it whole heartily. Stop holding back!

MY TESTAMONY

There was a time in my marriage that I was seriously considering throwing in the towel. I was frustrated and wanted to get some relief. One day during prayer, God confronted me with the question "what do I want?" My answer to the question caught me by surprise; I wanted my marriage to work. Next the Lord asked me "Then why are you contradicting yourself?" He made it obvious to me that I was contradicting myself. My actions and heart were not lining up with my own desire. It was clear to me then; I was to act like I love my wife regardless of how I feel or how she responded. The focus was that I could not contradict myself for any reason.

I committed to love my wife and stop holding back. I would not allow myself to use the excuse of her actions or inactions to influence as to how I was going to respond. Surprisingly enough, I was liberated from the frustration of contradicting myself. I realized then that my peace is centered on my actions and whether they agree with my heart or not. This was such a relief that I began to respond to her according to my own heart and not her behavior.

The better I get at following my own heart, the easier life gets for me. This has also provoked a change in my wife's behavior as well.

NOTE! I do not condone physical violence. If this exists, you must physically separate yourself from the situation and insist on counseling.

Men, you don't like to be treated harshly by your wives. I get it. But the greatest offense you can endure is when you allow your wife to dictate how you are going to love her. Trust me on this one... Stop contradicting yourself!

If you are dealing with emotional abuse, read this book and do the challenges (I know what I'm suggesting is difficult). Then after the challenges, you tell her that you would like her to read some information you have for her (say this in a whisper). (The information is my book, The Wife's Secret

Weapon). She will most likely be compelled because of the core needs you have met. Like you, I will teach her how to meet your core needs.

The influence is on your side of the court now. You have a huge advantage over the situation now. Once you start the challenges you will see what I'm talking about.

OK! You're probably thinking "My wife is not going to read a book written by a man on how to treat her husband!" Don't be so sure. If you do as much of the challenges as physically possible; you will be surprised at what she would be willing to do for you.

6

THE RELATOR & THE WARRIOR

Men, have you ever found yourself catching the last part of your wife's sentence? Have you found yourself frustrated because you feel like she wants you to sit on the edge of your seat at all times so that you don't miss what she is saying? I believe I can help you with this.

Women are verbally stimulated. Your wife can be performing all sorts of tasks with plenty of noise going on and someone can enter the area and say something totally off subject and she will hear clearly what was said. This is because women are verbally stimulated. They have such a heightened awareness for speech, they naturally tune to it immediately. Just like when a doctor takes a rubber mallet and hits your knee and you kick your leg involuntarily. It is her reflex. It is a reflex for women to tune in so keenly at the first sign of verbal communication. This is because God made them an expresser.

Your wife is also a relater! Is it any wonder why she wants to develop your relationship and feels that talking things out draws you closer? The truth is, when two people can talk things over, they will become more entwined with the other person.   The   relationship   is   stronger.   Try   to   be understanding if you wife treats you like you are verbally stimulated. We (men and women) have a proclivity to think we all function the same as us.

Wives gain strength from talking with you and hearing about your visions and plans for the future. She is very interested in what you have to say about her too. Make sure that you pour into her strengths more than you do her weaknesses. Please remember that you were not placed in her life to change her. She was placed in your life to balance you out.

I believe God put in women the need to discuss things and to develop relationships with you. The challenge is that men are not verbally stimulated and we are not expressers.

Men are warriors. They thrive on winning and success. They are built for the battle field and they have a reflex of their own. You see, men need to be able to ward off attacks and aggressive behavior. This is why God equipped men with what I call the wall. Yes, the wall has come between many a foe to allow the man to continue on with his daily business unscathed. Just as women are unaware of how keenly they pick up conversation, the men are unaware of how quickly their wall is deployed. Both men and women have a unique reflex.

This is why our wives get so frustrated with us because our wall comes up and they can tell that they didn't get through. Men, know that your wall has stopped many good things from getting to you. It is not your fault that the wall exists and that it deploys often. However, I would call you to work on controlling this reflex so that your wife can have access to your heart. She will treat it with great care.

As a warrior, we cannot allow our emotions to get involved while in battle. It would ensure defeat and the greater cause would be defenseless. This is why the wall is so necessary. On the balance of things, we must practice taking off our armor when we get home so that we don't accidently cut our wives with our sword. If that means establishing a few minutes when you get home to decompress before you come out to be with your wife, then coordinate it with her.

WHAT CAUSES THE WALL TO ACTIVATE?

Activating your wall can occur with the smallest peep of your wife's voice or only when she starts shouting. It can also be activated when there is tension between you two. It differs from man to man and the circumstances. It does not mean that you are unwilling to listen, it just means the wall was activated accidently or on purpose for defensive reasons. Remember that this is purely a reflex and most men are unaware that they have this wall. We have had it all our life and it is our normal. I believe that signs of the wall occur at a very young age. When a mother has to repeat herself to her son; this is a good sign of the wall being present.

Once the wall is activated, you can learn to deactivate it for your wife. It takes practice but you can do it.

One way to deactivate the wall is to ask your wife to touch you and whisper what she has to say. Tell her that she is very important and you can hear her better when she touches you and whispers it to you. Be sure to smile and whisper yourself if you have to. It's OK to chuckle while trying to deal with your wall. Have Fun!

King David was a mighty man of God! He was a warrior and known for the tens of thousands of enemies he destroyed. The bible also records him as being a man after God's own heart. Judging by his many wives and concubines, I would say that he was also a very good lover.

My point here is that we warriors can be just as successful at showing compassion to our wives and family as we are slaying our enemies. Remember to develop a different type of "you" when you are home. One that loves and chooses to serve your wife and children while with the family. This will make you very successful spiritually, emotionally and professionally.

7

STOP SHOUTING!
I can't hear you.

When a man raises his voice to his wife, he is doing more damage than he realizes. Louder does not mean that she will get your point any better. But she will be hurt by your tone and volume. At that point the message is not even heard because she is so overwhelmed by your boisterous presentation. You might as well be speaking in another language.

In many countries the culture today is to speak up! Be heard! Voice your opinion! Be the loudest voice in the crowd! We are also duped to believe that we are getting our message across to the person when we are shouting. Nothing could be further from the truth. Fact is, the louder you get, the less people listen.

The loudest person in a public argument will always be viewed by others as the one in the wrong. When a married couple argues in public, they dishonor one another. If the husband is shouting, he presents himself to the public as an insensitive husband that no woman would ever want. If the wife is shouting in public, she is viewed as a brute and sympathy will go towards the husband. Eventually, each will be hurt by how they were humiliated. When an issue arises that could escalate to an argument, tell your spouse that you can discuss this later. Remember that children fight in public.

When you are communicating with your wife, be aware that she was designed to receive from you and give it back a thousand fold. Keeping calm and staying patient plants seeds of endearment that comes back to you in spades. Proverbs says:

Pr 15:1 ¶ A soft answer turneth away wrath: but grievous words stir up anger.

Spend more time whispering to your wife. You will love her responses as it will disarm her. You will like it too.

PRINCIPLE: Being right and delivering your point incorrectly is just as bad as being wrong. You will get the same results as being wrong.

It's your choice really. You can satisfy your flesh by yelling at your wife and children; never getting your point across and never resolving the issue. It will repeat often as if you never said anything. OR, you can whisper and fix the problem; not having to deal with it so often.

I'm lazy, I'd rather save myself the time and effort by speaking softly so I can press on.

8

WHAT DOES A
WOMAN NEED?

Like you, your wife has core needs that must be met in order for your relationship to thrive. This book is written for you; rest assured that I will be covering your core needs with her in "The Wife's Secret Weapon".

In order to better understand the needs of a woman, let's cover needs and wants. I cover this with all my study cases so that they understand the difference between a need and a want. Your wife needs for you to understand that there are several needs a woman has that you can provide and that these are not wants. Below is a list of some needs and wants, I think that you will agree with my list:

NEEDS

Air   Water

Food   Clothes

WANTS

Nice Home   Expensive Car

The Best Tools

Your wife's needs are listed below in the order of precedence to her. You'll want to try to meet them with the same level of importance.

NEED #1

To be gently lead in the things of God.

Women are very receptive to spiritual things. This would mean that you approach her and ask her if she would like to pray with you. If she accepts, just be yourself, the point here is that you were willing to pray with her.

Maybe you can ask her if she would like to read the bible together. Start in the New Testament in Mark and read through John and then go back through them again; starting with Matthew.

Ask her what the chapter meant to her and if you see something else mention it. The bible is a living document; meaning that it speaks to hearts on what they need at the time. So two people can read the same chapter and get something totally different. This is a good thing. By listening to what she gets out of it; you can see a little more into her heart and with what she is dealing. This is vital if you are going to be empathetic to her. You must be empathetic!!!!

This is not for you to become a dictatorship. This is you caring enough to join with her to learn how to pray together and trust in God together. It is acceptable for you to tell her that you don't know what you are doing but you want to do this with her.

The previous approach is much better than you acting like you know what you are doing. Trust me when I tell you, you really don't know what you are doing. So, don't fake it. It is very good if you can tell your wife that you really don't know what you are doing but you want to pray with her.

NEED #2

To be heard.

Remember that your wife is an expresser? She gets relief from stress talking about it. You meet this need perfectly when you listen to her.

HERE IS A WORD PICTURE

Imagine that you have a beautiful brand new white truck and for some reason, your wife drives it to work every day.

One day she pulls up with the truck loaded with manure. Your response is total outrage because she has soiled your nice new truck! As you come outside to express your frustration, you see her shoveling the manure onto the lawn. You begin to let her know what she has done is unacceptable with no uncertain terms. In response, she drops what she is doing and goes into the house.

The rest of the night, the tension is thick in the air, and she has no intentions of you getting close to her.

The next day she returns from work with twice the amount of manure on the truck and as she begins to shovel the manure onto the lawn, you go outside and rail on her again and she responds as she did before.

The following day she returns with the truck so loaded down that, once she parks it on the driveway, it can no longer move. She is also unable to be of any kindness to you because she is concerned about cleaning the truck and getting it back to its pristine condition.

HERE IS THE ANALAGY OF THIS WORD PICTURE:

Every time your wife starts to share with you her issues of the day, she is driving the truck full of manure into the drive way. As she continues to talk to you, she is cleaning the truck. If she is able to clean the truck, then she can immediately go on to the other needs of the family.

You as the husband can play an important role in the success and speed of this process. If you listen proactively, it is as if you got a shovel and helped clean the truck. She will be able to respond to you very positively once the burden of the truck is gone.

So how do you respond proactively? Contrary to our natural desire to fix problems, your wife really needs you to listen and don't try to make suggestions on what she should do. Sometimes I respond with: "Well babe, you handled that better than I would have. I'm proud of you because I think I would have said something that would have gotten me fired!"

Most women have a truck that gets filled all day and every day. Their process of unloading is talking it out. If you can just picture your wife shoveling off her truck when she begins to tell you the negative things, then you might see some personal benefit in listening.

Actually, most women are very positive. This process of expressing the negative feelings and events allows them to keep from harboring such negativity. You don't need to respond, answer or fix any of these problems. Just listen. If you listen long enough, you'll hear her say out of the same breath "You know, it was a pretty good day anyway!". It's easier for her to appreciate the brand new truck if it's not laden with manure.

This is not about complaining. It's about how most women need to process the issues of the day to stay on the positive side of things. She will find a way to get to the positive side. Whoever becomes responsible for listening to her will reap a greater return than the investment. I hope the husband decides to be the investor.

If you're real good, you can work on listening for approximately 15 minutes a day and the grass will be greener on your side of the fence.

I will admit that sometimes I don't know if my wife wants me to listen, give an opinion or take action. Instead of trying to guess, I ask her "do you want me to be a listener, give my opinion or take action?" She will tell me and I feel successful because I am doing what she needs me to do. I, like every other man, don't like getting it wrong with my wife.

Men, you're your most effective tool is in listening without judging. When a man does this, he becomes the true warrior to his wife. Because she is an expresser, you allowing her to get the pressure off will make you the hero every time. Men, show me a man who gets all the lovin he can handle and I'll show you a woman who has no stress!

One final thought, if you were to say all the thoughts you think when you are dealing with stress, it would sound exactly like your wife.... So, give them a break; don't judge. And when she finishes destressing, wipe the board clean and forget about it; just as you do with your thoughts during stressful times.

NEED #3

To be loved.

A woman who is belittled by her husband will incubate negativity and give birth to a very ugly child and mother. This can range from embarrassing her in public to ridicule when you are home. The following scripture has been used to bash men for years and this is not my intent. However if we are going to cover this from a biblical perspective, then we must be aware of what the scriptures share.

Eph 5:25 Husbands, love your wives, even as Christ also loved the church, and gave himself for it;

This love is the sacrificial love (agape) that was discussed earlier. We are to give ourselves to our marriage for our wives.

Spending time with her, like a date night, honors her. It says to her that she is so important that a specific day each week is put aside for you to laugh and have fun together. A date night on a weekly basis is a very powerful tool to keep things going well. Do it. Even if it consists of a peanut butter and jelly sandwich and a moment alone; start somewhere. You can ask her for ideas. I think she will love that. Make it mandatory for you! Don't let things get in the way of this. You missing a date night should be rare and with both of you agreeing on it.

Contrary to popular belief, negative comments and jokes about your wife when she is not with you brings a spirit of disrespect and she will respond to you when you bring that home. She may not be able to identify it but she will respond to it. Bank on it!

NEED #4

To be accepted as she is.

Your wife may have a few things she needs to work on but she knows when you are trying to change her. There is a difference between trying to change her and drawing out of her the woman you see inside. Loving your wife with smiles and soft touches (nonsexual touches) will cause her to trust you more and pull out the loving woman in her. She is keenly aware that she needs to get better in some areas. Your job is to love her and support her like Christ does for us. Jesus looks past the mess and blesses us. As the head of the house, it is your responsibility to give the family a good vision of the Father in heaven. You must choose, daily if necessary, to not let your frustrations dictate to you how you are going to love her. Jesus doesn't let our nasty disposition, selfish attitudes, and controlling ways change how He loves us.

Col 3:19 Husbands, love [your] wives, and be not bitter against them.

Ro 2:4 Or despisest thou the riches of his goodness and forbearance and longsuffering; not knowing that the goodness of God leadeth thee to repentance?

Romans above describe God's desire to be good to us so that we become so grateful that we repent for our bad thoughts, words or behavior. This is your assignment as well. Giving your wife better than she deserves is a powerful tool to help you bring her back to you. Please remember that I am speaking in regards to an adult dealing with another adult.

This reminds me of the story of a couple, married 37 years, who were in counseling. The wife tells the counselor that her husband doesn't love her. The counselor asks her why she believes that. She replied, "Because he never tells me!" The counselor asks the husband "Sir, is that true?" The husband answers "I told her that I loved her when I married her and I haven't changed my mind!"

Don't be that guy!

NEED #5

Security.

Your wife is looking for security. This covers physical security, emotional security, financial security, family security and marriage security.

It is imperative that you do not use the "D" word (divorce) when you are arguing. It tears at her security so that she will begin to stop trusting you in other areas as well. You do not want to have to recover from this type of mistake. If you have already done so, stop and pray that God intervene on your behalf to get past it.

Family security is you being the one who honors family values and expects all to follow suit. She is the nester and relational type of nature so you must rely on her to help you enforce this standard... This will honor her.

Financial security is not the same for all women, however, you should discuss with her what would make her feel secure financially and plan with her accordingly.

Emotional Security is you telling her that you love her every day. You should tell her how much you love her. Never tell her that you love her because of .... This implies to her that if that is gone, so is your love. You want to convey to her that you don't know why you love her, you just do. This means that she can't lose it by changing in any way. As you meet these other needs, she will see you showing her that you love her.

Physical Security has to do with a place to stay and good transportation. Making sure that she has a reliable car and a sound home over her head is a very powerful thing when all the other needs are being meet as well.

NEED #6

Sex

Women do like sex. They enjoy an orgasm as well as anyone else. Your job is to learn what works for her and give it to her. Your body was designed to gain maximum pleasure from sex when your wife is gaining pleasure. If you focus on meeting her needs, you will be satisfied as well.

1 Peter 3:7 Likewise, ye husbands, dwell with them according to knowledge, giving honour unto the wife, as unto the weaker vessel, and as being heirs together of the grace of life; that your prayers be not hindered.

Let me say here that this scripture forced me into an important question: What knowledge is this scripture talking about? After prayer and learning these principles, I believe the answer is the knowledge that the wife teaches the husband. Who better to teach you how to dwell with her? Personally, I am more concerned with what my wife likes than what other women like.

Talk with your wife during sex. Ask her if she likes what you are doing. Ask her what she would like from you. If she doesn't know, help her by starting somewhere. Tell her that you really think it's sexy when she likes what you do for her. She will want to know that you like it when she is enjoying it. You will too.

So what is allowed and not allowed in the marriage bed? I get asked this often. My best advice is this; the bible says:

Heb 13:4 Marriage [is] honourable in all, and the bed undefiled: but whoremongers and adulterers God will judge.

Please try to stay with the natural use of the body. Unnatural uses of the body are contradictory to God's design and purpose. However, my main guidance is: Both of you must be in agreement.

Look up Romans 1:16-27 in your bible.

Just so that I know you know, here are some things to know. There are always exceptions, however, generally these hold true for most. She and/or you may not know this so discuss it while you touch her and whisper.

- Women can have more than one orgasm. They may not need to rest to go again. The wife going for another can be very exciting.
- Men can have more than one orgasm. You may need to ask for a minute before you start again. But you don't always have to stop completely.
- Men love to hear positive feedback during sex. This is not the time for an expresser to get quiet. You want to win with her and feedback helps you please her; even if it is in whispers and soft moans. Encourage your wife to at least whisper what she likes. BE TEACHABLE!
- Some men may fall asleep after sex. Chemically it is not unusual. According to LiveScience, an article entitled "Why do guys get sleepy after sex?"

Research shows that during ejaculation, men release a cocktail of brain chemicals, including norepinephrine, serotonin, oxytocin, vasopressin, nitric oxide (NO), and the hormone prolactin. The release of prolactin is linked to the feeling of sexual satisfaction, and it also mediates the "recovery time" that men are well aware of—the time a guy must wait before "giving it another go." Studies have also shown that men deficient in prolactin have faster recovery times.

Prolactin levels are naturally higher during sleep, and animals injected with the chemical become tired immediately. This suggests a strong link between prolactin and sleep, so it's likely that the hormone's release during orgasm causes men to feel sleepy.

Oxytocin and vasopressin, two other chemicals released during orgasm, are also associated with sleep. Their release frequently accompanies that of melatonin, the primary hormone that regulates our body clocks. Oxytocin is also thought to reduce stress levels, which again could lead to relaxation and sleepiness.
(article: http://www.livescience.com/32445-why-do-guys-get-sleepy-after-sex.html)

The art of learning is repetition. So, practice, practice, practice! ☺

HOW MUCH IS TOO MUCH SEX

This question comes up a lot and I would like to say that fourteen times a day is ok if you both agree to it. To find the right balance for your relationship, I recommend the pendulum effect. A pendulum finds the center (or balance) by swinging to extremes.

What this means is try to have more sex than you both can possibly stand and then go for a while until someone wants some. Somewhere in there is your balance.

SAYING NO TO SEX

The bible shares that the only time to avoid sex is for a time of fasting and prayer; of which both of you have agreed on. Men, if you are lead to go on a fast, tell her so and for how long. The bible says that you are to come together immediately after to keep the enemy from getting in. So, if you end your fasting and prayer early, let your wife know and talk about when you can come together.

1Corinthians 7:5 Defraud ye not one the other, except [it be] with consent for a time, that ye may give yourselves to fasting and prayer; and come together again, that Satan tempt you not for your incontinency.

Sometimes you are just too exhausted for sex and you are asking for mercy. So how do you tell her that you don't want to have sex when she asks? Use your soft voice or whisper and tell her that you enjoy having sex with her but you are so tired and would love to take a raincheck. Then promise her when you can have sex. DANGER! You must keep your word. Empty promises will create suspicion and doubt about the relationship. If something comes up that prevents you from keeping your promise, be the first one to bring it up and tell her in a playful way when you can. Don't delay too many times and always be the first one to bring it up. This will let her know that she is still sexy to you and that you haven't forgotten her.

If she insists on sex, try your best to rock her world while you get yours. No sense in getting into it without a happy ending for all.

If you are in a balanced sex life, the interruptions will be easily tolerated. If the interruptions are not easily tolerated, that may be an indication for sex more often.

Sex is very beneficial for both the male and female. Don't discard the power of the "quickie" either. It brings you both as physically close as possible. Spiritually, it increases your bond. Emotionally, it helps you maintain some balance. Finally, biologically, it is healthy for you both.

Remember that sex is a very spiritual event between a husband and wife. It not only makes you one in the flesh, it links you both closer in the soul and spirit. Learning to serve one another in bed is very powerful.

9

TAKE THE
CHALLENGE!

The purpose of these challenges is to tremendously increase your success in dealing with your wife and find the joy that you seek with your relationship.

Don't be surprised at the dramatic changes you will see in a relatively short time as you do these challenges.

Now would be a good time to go over the rules of engagement.

1. You do not tell her where you are getting these ideas. If she asks, simply say "Can't a husband love on his wife?"

    Here is the fun part! When you say that to her, she is thinking that if she says no, you will stop doing what you are doing and she doesn't want that. If she says yes, then she cannot continue to ask about the sudden changes. You win!!! Have fun with this because her curiosity will be peaked to know what is going on.

2. You cannot tell her about this book until you have completed all the challenges and waited for the specified time afterward.

   You want to allow her to marinate over the last event so that you can peak her interest.

3. Try to do all the challenges as given to you with as little deviation as possible.

4. Have Fun!!!!

   Throughout the challenges, you get to watch your wife try to figure out what exactly is going on. She loves what you're doing but she can't connect the dots on how all this came about. For a woman, this will cause her to do a lot of thinking about you. You will get to enjoy the struggle you see on her face… Lots of fun for you!!!!

   Incidentally, the change will make her want to say "I don't know who you are but what have you done with my husband!" Yet it will be very appealing to her.

So let's get busy!

CHALLENGE #1

Day 1:

Privately sit down beside her, and whisper the following:

"You know how you talk about things to get relief from stress? Well I have to think about things and that is how I deal with my stress. So, when I become quieter, I am most likely dealing with stress. I'm not mad at you and the stress could be job related. I will most likely tell you about it once my stress is dealt with.

If you don't know if I'm dealing with stress, you can ask me if I need some time to think."

Next: Tell her if you don't mind if she touches you or sits with you while you are thinking. Or tell her you just need some alone time when you are thinking.

WHAT IS GOING ON WITH HER?

At this point she is not sure what just happened. You did something different, she liked it but she can't figure out where this came from. She'll think about it for the next day or so. Her first thought may be that it was a fluke and it won't happen again. She is looking for permanent change so be consistent with this.

WHAT IS IN IT FOR YOU?

You have just begun the first seed of mystery with her. Congratulations! Trust me when I tell you that this will fester; especially as the days go by.

She will appreciate that you realize that she needs to talk about things to get the same relief from stress. She will also learn that you don't deal with stress the same way. This will make her less defensive when you get quieter. Now we are in a Win – Win situation.

CHALLENGE #2

Day 2:

(In a whisper) Tell your wife that you realize that she needs to talk to deal with stress. Tell her that you want to practice listening to her without interrupting and giving advice on how to fix it. Ask her to be patient with you as you perfect this skill. If you interrupt, apologize and ask her to continue.

Understand that listening is doing something. Something HUGE! So, learn to fight that reflex that wants to jump in and solve the problem.

You may need to ask her from time to time if she needs to vent or is she asking for some input.

Here are some statements that are usually acceptable while you listen; she does not want you to just sit there:

I understand.

I would have done the same thing or worse.

You did the right thing.

I'm proud of you.

That's my baby!

I'm sorry you had to go through that.

Basically, these statements are empathetic, sympathetic, understanding and they validate that she makes good decisions. She will always appreciate validation from her husband more than anywhere else.

WHAT IS IN IT FOR YOU?

You are positioning yourself as a source of relief from stress for her. Women are drawn to this source like a moth to a flame. This is also a good way to prevent your wife from having an affair. If she knows that she can come to you (the one she loves) and get relief, she will never stray.

Also, if her stress is gone, she can minister to your needs (need I say more?) The more often you spend time listening, the less time it will take for her to press on with other needs. So if at first, she runs long winded for a few days, she was in desperate need for some relief.

CHALLENGE #3

Day 5 or there about:

After spending several days becoming her source of stress relief, have your wife sit down somewhere where you can wash her feet. Get a towel and a pan with warm water; put a couple of drops of olive oil in the water. Kneel down and wash her feet. Take the time to message the oil into her feet. While doing so, tell her how much you love her and appreciate her for who she is and what she does for you and the family. Be specific and general in your appreciation.

When you have dried her feet, tell her "**You Are My Queen**". Do not misquote this.

If you have to persuade her, whisper. Tell her that you need to. If she insists, tell her that it would hurt your feelings if she denies you.

Don't be afraid to kneel at her feet, you are not enabling her to be over you. She may even be embarrassed. She will like it because it will convey that you value her.

Jesus washed his disciple's feet, he then asked them to wash others.

WHAT IS GOING ON WITH HER?

She will most likely be overwhelmed, embarrassed or even blush. She may not be used to you ministering to her need for care and affection at such a deep level. But it will bless her dramatically in your favor.

DO NOT use this as a precursor for sex. In fact, set in your mind that you will not initiate sex tonight because you do not want her to associate this as a way for you to get what you want. However, if she initiates sex, give her what she wants.

WHAT IS IN IT FOR YOU?

When you said to her "You Are My Queen", she will be honored and blessed to know that you place her so high in your priorities. Consequently, you win!!!

You are actually showing her how you want to handle her heart by handling her feet. This may pull out of her more conversation. If so, let her have this time. You'll be glad you did.

CHALLENGE #4

The next day:

Tell Her!

Pray this first:

> Lord Jesus, move on my wife when I tell her about the book I want her to read. And let her read the book and put to practice what she has learned. In Jesus Name, Amen

Now you may tell her where you got these ideas from. Ask her if she liked them and if they helped make the relationship better. Also, tell her that you have a book for her to read that was written by the same author (The Wife's Secret Weapon). She will be most willing to read this book after her experience with you over the past week or so.

CHALLENGE #5

Retrain yourself to whisper more often; especially when you are angry or emotional. This will have a dramatic effect on her and prove to be more beneficial for you. She will get it and respond much better than if you put a voice to your anger.

WHAT IS GOING ON WITH HER?

She will become less defensive and will hear you much better. Whispering takes the distraction of tones out of the picture and you will be less frustrated in trying to communicate.

WHAT IS IN IT FOR YOU?

You will have more peace and pleasure in your house and it will be less effort for you to correct issues as they arise. Now you two can mature together and truly become one.

<u>FINALLY</u>

Make these challenges a regular staple in your relationship. They are guaranteed to increase and maintain the two of you together.

I wish you all the success in the world... I wish you Jesus!

10

YOUR ROLE

FROM A BIBLICAL PERSPECTIVE

Understanding your role as a husband is imperative if you are to be successful in your relationship. Below is a scriptural basis on which to understand your role and I will also try to convey the proper mindset and approach you should take as a husband. Some of these scriptures are self-explanatory. So, I will not comment on those.

1Pe 5:5 ¶ Likewise, ye younger, submit yourselves unto the elder. Yea, all [of you] **be subject one to another**, and be clothed with humility: for God resisteth the proud, and giveth grace to the humble.

The scripture above clearly delineates that Husbands and Wives should be subject to each other. This means that even though God has placed the man as the head of the family, he must be subject to his wife.

The Greek word for Subject is **υποτασσω** hupotasso (pronounced hoop-ot-as'-so) meaning to submit one's self. It implies that the husband and wife must place themselves in subject to each other. Notice that it does not say that they make the other submit. Basically, you are required to place yourself under submission.

It also means:

> to submit to one's control
>
> to yield to one's admonition or advice
>
> to obey, be subject

Below is a scripture that men need to understand in a more perfect way.

1 Peter 3:1 ¶ Likewise, ye wives, be in subjection to your own husbands; that, if any obey not the word, they also may without the word be won by the conversation of the wives; **2** While they behold your chaste conversation coupled with fear. **3** Whose adorning let it not be that outward adorning of plaiting the hair, and of wearing of gold, or of putting on of apparel; **4** But let it be the hidden man of the heart, in that which is not corruptible, even the ornament of a meek and quiet spirit, which is in the sight of God of great price. **5** For after this manner in the old time the holy women also, who trusted in God, adorned themselves, being in subjection unto their own husbands: **6** Even as Sara obeyed Abraham, calling him lord: whose daughters ye are, as long as ye do well, and are not afraid with any amazement. **7** Likewise, ye husbands, dwell with them according to knowledge, giving honour unto the wife, as unto the weaker vessel, and as being heirs together of the grace of life; that your prayers be not hindered.

Verse 3 speaks of a woman coupling fear with their chaste conversation. Men, this is the fear of the Lord. If you are doing things to provoke fear in your wife, you are very far from grace and favor of the Lord Jesus Christ.

Verse 4 through 6 is giving priority and importance for women to concentrate on keeping a pure heart first, not telling women to avoid wearing gold and silver.

Verse 7 does not claim that women are weaker; it directs men to give honor to the wife AS the weaker vessel. It also instructs the men that when they do this their prayers won't be hindered.

Col 3:19 Husbands, love [your] wives, and be not bitter against them.

Eph 5:25 Husbands, love your wives, even as Christ also loved the church, and gave himself for it;

There are many more references but I think that these clearly identify the role of the Husband and the role of the Wife from a biblical perspective.

I would like to emphasize that marriage God's way provides a 100% chance of success.

HERE IS A GOOD MINDSET

If you have to tell your wife that you are the head, you have lost your position of authority.

If you have to tell your wife to submit, you have lost your authority and proven that you have given her nothing to submit to.

Leadership is a lifestyle of constantly displaying the love, grace and patience to your wife as Christ affords you. You must lead by example and allow your wife the option not to follow. You are the head of the household. You are responsible for the condition of your marriage. If God leads you to do something, tell your wife and tell her that you understand if she does not agree or chooses not to comply.

A true leader does what they know God has called them to do and looks behind them to notice there are followers. The moment you must persuade someone to go along, you are not leading and you will be forced to spend the same energy on a regular basis.

Jesus led by example. He loved the Jews and Gentiles and it changed their lives. Love is a very powerful weapon; More powerful than anger, wrath and physical intimidation.

PUT YOUR SWORD DOWN

When you come home, take all your armor off! Try to greet your family with an excited voice every time you see them. Don't come home with the anticipation that there will be an argument. If you expect it, it will come! Even if the previous encounter was difficult, start the next one with a new excitement. Men FAKE THIS IF YOU HAVE TO! This is part of the process of putting your sword down so you don't accidently poke or cut a member of your family.

All men feel unappreciated at times. But you are supposed to be like Jesus to your family. So serve them and stop expecting them to serve you all the time. Jesus, The Son Of God, served people, washed their feet, prayed for them, and encouraged them. You must do the same. The more you focus on being unappreciated, the more you will be miserable. When your priorities are right, your joy will be right.

Pastor Philip Campbell put it best!

> J O Y
>
> J = Jesus First
>
> O = Others Next (Family)
>
> Y = Yourself last
>
> Selfish people are never happy and never have joy.

As a husband, pray for your wife and children. Your prayers will be heard by God as you are the point of contact for the family. Ask God to guide your wife and children into the things of God. This is a loaded prayer as God desires to see the family blessed and joyous.

11

THE TOOL BOX

USING THE RIGHT TOOL FOR THE JOB

Everybody understands what it's like to try to do something with inadequate tools. If they have the right tools, the task is completed much more efficiently and allows one to move on to other tasks. More powerfully is having the right tools and knowing how to apply them effectively. Many times, in our profession, we engage in training on how to apply our tools more effectively. My question to you is, how much effort do you apply yourself to learn how to use your God given tools for relationships?

Most men know what it's like to try to use pliers to unscrew a cross head screw. A Phillips screwdriver would not only be the right tool, it would take less time to complete the task. Ask any mechanic today and they will tell you to never underestimate the power of having the right tool for the job. The right tool for the job will speed up the process and make it much easier. In fact, many mechanics go to school to learn how to apply the tools more effectively.

My goal is to give you more effective tools with your spouse and show you how to use them more effectively. In the long run, you will save time and energy as you master these skills. So, let's begin!

THE DYNAMICS OF MARRIAGE

There are many dynamics in a marriage that go unaddressed before, during or after a marriage. It is my desire to cover a few of them in this chapter. I hope that covering these facets will become powerful tools for you.

I used to hear people say that marriage is hard work but I never really understood that. Now I have come to know that there are dynamics in my marriage that I strive to improve on so that my wife and I can enjoy our marriage. I will never tell you that we have perfected everything, however I will tell you that we are constantly working on it; privately and together. I will never tell you that this is easy but I will tell you that it is rewarding.

It is best to look at this as a work in progress for the rest of your life. Granted, the art of learning is repetition, and through constant use, you will be very successful. However, you must never allow yourself to be satisfied with what you have achieved. It is imperative that you continue to perfect your skills; regardless of your current success.

MARRIAGE IS AN ENTITY ALL OF ITS OWN

There are four entities in a marriage:

God, Marriage, The Man, and The Woman

According to God, marriage is not an action or a fad. It is a binding covenant between a man and a woman. With God, all covenants are living testaments to something greater than the two who entered into it. When God entered into a covenant with Abraham, He kept his word. When God told Abraham that he would be the father of many nations, God entered into a covenant with Abraham and it became so. All throughout the bible, covenants were taken very seriously by God and man. Today, covenants are just as weighty as they were then. There are powerful forces at work when we enter into a covenant. My prayer is that you realize the power behind your covenant of marriage.

If we treat marriage like a living entity, then we will make decisions and govern ourselves for the sake of the marriage and Jesus Christ; even when we lack interest.

Remember that your priority is God first, your spouse, then children, yourself, and finally your extended family and friends. Any time this order is changed, your walk will become a lot harder. Also, your children are learning from you how to prioritize family. It is healthy for them to see you make their father more important; there is a sense of security they derive from this.

Finally, the greatest thing you can do as a husband is pray for your family to be touched by God in a greater measure. I recommend laying your hands on them and pray a blessing over them. As the head, you have a very powerful anointing to impart into you your wife and children.

Tool #1

Trust Is Earned!

Trust is earned, not given away freely. I had a car salesman, of whom I have never met, ask me "don't you trust me?". I replied with the above sentence.

Trust is also multilevel. My trust with a car salesman requires minimal verification compared to a relationship with someone I call my friend. Even more is required for my spouse. It was former president Ronald Reagan who said "Trust but verify!"

Verification is vital to deep trust. Like an onion, the more your spouse trusts you, the more they will reveal their heart to you. I remember one incident where my wife told me something about herself that took ten years of marriage to earn her trust.

So, it's our responsibility to confirm our loyalty to our spouse anytime they ask us where we've been, who we're speaking with on the phone, texting, reading, or looking at on the computer/TV. The more they ask, the more opportunity we have to earn more trust. This is especially important if there have been some incidences that have created mistrust.

WARNING! Any defensive response or sign of impatience with the questions will most likely be interpreted as guilt of wrong doing.

If you have lost your spouse's trust, you can earn it back but it will take some time and humility on your part. The more trust that you have lost, the more time and humility it will require.

If you are now asking "How long do I have to endure the questions?" It may be time to see a pastor who can help you and your spouse address any issues peculiar to your situation. I recommend someone I trust...

Pastor Anthony McMillan is the Founder and CEO of HD Relationships. He is also the Senior Pastor of Life Church, Pensacola, Florida. His given gift from God is helping relationships reach a level of High Definition. Take time to look them up on Facebook or online. You'll be glad that you did!

Tool #2

Dictionaries
HIS & HERS & THEIRS

Early in my marriage, my wife and I would go out on a date as we still do. But back then, once we got home, I would say "Honey I had a Fantastic Time!" She would reply "It was Alright." My ego would take a major hit. Many date nights were ruined by the ensuing arguments because I thought she was saying that she didn't enjoy herself when I witnessed her smiles and laughter. Not to mention my pride was hurt because I thought I did good.

Finally, God made it painfully clear that maybe she was saying something different than what I thought. So after another date night, I said the same thing and she replied the same way. But this time, I stopped and said "Babe, when I was growing up, alright meant that I was just getting by. Is that what you mean?" To my surprise, she said "No, alright was like saying awesome."

Right then I realized that all this time we were in, what I like to call, violent agreement. We were saying the same thing with different words.

Now when she says "alright" I think: That's right! I'm the Man!!!

This is where the dictionary principle comes in.

When you were a child, for survival reasons, you adopted your parent's terms and definitions. You had no choice because it was the only game in town for you to learn how to communicate. No getting around this one.

However, over time, you have become so comfortable with your dictionary of terms that you are tempted to assume that everyone around you has the same dictionary. Nothing could be further from the truth.

When two people from two different families get married, there is an inevitable collision of terms about to take place. How does one protect themselves from this type of conflict? It is very easy.

Remember to ask what the other person means before you assume that they mean your negative definition. Take the time to explain to them what it means to you. Then ask them for their definition.

You have just begun creating a third dictionary. This dictionary is unique because it connects two different words to one meaning.

Sometimes, my wife will say fantastic for me. This carries a double blessing: she had a great time and she wanted to use my word to put a little extra with it…. Nice huh?

If you fail to stay calm and investigate the meaning. You will not move forward in understanding each other and the subject at hand will come up again. Don't be as slow as I was; get it right as soon as possible. It will save you a huge amount of time and effort. Trust me on this one!

Tool #3

I Need…. I Need

For years, I would tell my wife that I needed something from her and she would go right in to telling me what she needed from me. This used to frustrate me because I would end up feeling like she was retorting back an unmet need that I have yet to provide. It would make me feel that we are at a stalemate; until you meet my needs, I won't meet yours. I would end up thinking; I am going to stop telling her my needs because she just keeps firing back at me.

Finally, one day, I explained to her how I felt when she did that and that is when I got a new revelation.

She wasn't discounting my need; she was getting into the mode of sharing needs. This is how she put it: She said "When I talk to my sisters, someone would say that they need to get a new blouse. Then another would say that they need to get a couch for the family room and another would say that they need to get their car cleaned." My wife thought I was going into a sharing needs conversation so she chimed in.

You may be sharing a need with your spouse and they may respond by sharing a need of theirs. It may be that they are not retorting with their unmet need. The underlying issue here may be: you could have taken care of that need and did not; this could make you a little defensive.

HOW TO ADDRESS YOUR SPOUSE'S NEEDS

When your spouse starts off the need sharing conversation, address that need before you share your need. It even helps to ask them if they would like to hear ONE of your needs since we are on the subject. If the answer is no, then you should respond with "OK, maybe another time."

When I bring up one of my needs to my wife, I want her to respond to my need first. This makes me feel like she is listening and cares about my needs. Once she addresses my need, she can share her need. Try to keep it to one need at a time. If one person names off many needs, then the one listening may feel that they don't have a right to their need. That is unfair! Don't be that gal!

No matter how small the need, if your spouse mentions a need to you, you are responsible for treating that need with care. Celebrating your differences includes allowing each to share their needs; regardless of how great or small.

My wife places the knives in the silverware holder blade down because I told her that I didn't want anyone to get hurt reaching for a fork. This is one of my needs.

I try to help my wife with her projects around the house because that is one of her needs.

Tool #4

Customer Service

Not all customer service centers are open 24/7. However, if you want your wife's customer service center to stay open more often, you will need to keep your customer service center open as much as possible. If you are the first to open your customer service center for more hours, trust me when I tell you that it will pay big dividends!!!

You must try to meet your wife's need to talk and other needs as much as possible. You want to be the only customer service desk she uses when it comes to relieving stress. If you are the sole source of stress relief, you will be the benefactor of all her love. In other words, her customer service desk will be open for longer hours. Remember that women are not physically and visually stimulated as men.

Practice keeping the wall down; You can do it. A sword swallower practice fighting the gag reflex until it is second nature to him. With practice, you will be able to control the wall at will.

Listening is not the only way your wife gets pleasure from you. She is extremely interested in how you feel. Yes, men, I said the "F" word. She will love hearing you talk about how you feel about her, your job, your family, your kids, your lawn etc.... Communication to her is a form of intimacy. Learn to talk with her about you from an emotional point of view. Now before you say that you are not emotional, I want to remind you that anger is an emotion, frustration is an emotion, joy, laughter and warm feelings are also emotions. You are emotional. Make sure that your wife isn't exposed to only the negative emotions that you have. It's OK to start off the conversation with "I'm new to sharing my feelings with words so be patient with me. I just want to share with you how I feel." She will love this and it makes her feel that you trust her with something that you have given to no one else.

If you want your wife's customer service center to stay open more often, you will need to use your tools. Women are verbally stimulated so you can begin a conversation with them very easily. Talking to your wife as if she were a man is the quickest way to close up shop. Maybe you will need to lower the volume of your voice. Or raise the pitch of your voice ever so slightly. Whispering can be very effective; especially if you are dealing with her sensitivity to your tone.

Your job is to keep your customer service window open as much as possible. This means that you must give your wife what she needs. Doing the challenges teaches you the core needs of your woman and how to meet them. The better you become at meeting them, the more influential you become with her. It's really a win-win situation.

Remember that customer service representatives try to meet their customer's needs and sometimes don't always agree with the customer. If this can be done in business, how much more should you do that to the one who committed to marry you.

Tool #5

Don't Assume You Know!

If you ever find yourself thinking "she did this because …". You are assuming that you know why she did something without asking her. The problem is when you are so convinced that you know what your wife means that you don't bother to ask her. This type of mindset will foster negative reinforcement about your wife and it will cloud your judgement of what really is coming from her heart. So, ask before you jump to conclusions.

Seeing the truth is harder when you have been hurt in the past from your childhood, other relationships and your wife. It's easy to be defensive once you have been hurt; too easy. One of the ways to heal and create a new mindset with your wife is to ask her what she meant by ….. Then it is your responsibility to take her at her word. In other words, you can't trust your beliefs; you must accept and adopt her explanation.

Early in our marriage, my wife would assume I meant one thing when I meant another. She wouldn't ask me what I meant and it would pile up and fester. I felt like I was being framed, tried, judged and sentenced without being allowed to have a defense. That is a helpless feeling.

My wife thought that I was blaming her for things when that was the furthest thing from my mind. Once she started asking me if I was blaming her, I was able to affirm that I wasn't. Over time, she began to know that my heart was not about blaming her. All because she kept asking until it wasn't a question.

My point here is, do not nail a meaning or motive on your wife until she has been given ample room to clarify her meaning. To clarify further, if you have repeated what she said over and over until she has not made any additions or continued to clarify, then she has been given ample room.

I ask that you leave room in your heart for her to clarify a misunderstanding or situation. No woman wants to purposely anger her husband. Besides, if you continue to allow her to clarify what she means, she will appreciate the maturity you are showing her.

Tool #6

Decisions

The 25th chapter of 1st Samuel shares a story of Nabal who refused to give David and his men provisions for the protection that they had provided. David was so angry that he prepared his men to destroy all the men in Nabal's charge. Abigail, Nabal's wife, heard of the situation and quickly loaded up provisions and met David and his men on their way to destroy Nabal.

1Sa 25:20 And it was [so, as] she rode on the ass, that she came down by the covert of the hill, and, behold, David and his men came down against her; and she met them.

1Sa 25:23 And when Abigail saw David, she hasted, and lighted off the ass, and fell before David on her face, and bowed herself to the ground, **24** And fell at his feet, and said, Upon me, my lord, [upon] me [let this] iniquity [be]: and let thine handmaid, I pray thee, speak in thine audience, and hear the words of thine handmaid.

1Sa 25:27 And now this blessing which thine handmaid hath brought unto my lord, let it even be given unto the young men that follow my lord. **28** I pray thee, forgive the trespass of thine handmaid: for the LORD will certainly make my lord a sure house; because my lord fighteth the battles of the LORD, and evil hath not been found in thee [all] thy days.

1Sa 25:30 And it shall come to pass, when the LORD shall have done to my lord according to all the good that he hath spoken concerning thee, and shall have appointed thee ruler over Israel; **31** That this shall be no grief unto thee, nor offence of heart unto my lord, either that thou hast shed blood causeless, or that my lord hath avenged himself: but when the LORD shall have dealt well with my lord, then remember thine handmaid.

David then answers this woman who honored him for who he is and who he will become:

1Sa 25:33 And blessed [be] thy advice, and blessed [be] thou, which hast kept me this day from coming to [shed] blood, and from avenging myself with mine own hand. **34** For in very deed, [as] the LORD God of Israel liveth, which hath kept me back from hurting thee, except thou hadst hasted and come to meet me, surely there had not been left unto Nabal by the morning light any that pisseth against the wall. **35** So David received of her hand [that] which she had brought him, and said unto her, Go up in peace to thine house; see, I have hearkened to thy voice, and have accepted thy person.

Your wife may not have the eloquence of Abigail but she is wired to see who you are and who you are to become. Including her in your decisions is the smartest thing you could ever do. Let me remind you:

Pr 21:1 ¶ The king's heart [is] in the hand of the LORD, [as] the rivers of water: he turneth it whithersoever he will.

This scripture not only speaks of one who rules a nation or a kingdom, it also speaks of authority over us. Did you notice that it didn't say that the authority over you had to be saved? It simply said that God will turn the king as He wills. So, you should pray to please God so that God will turn the authority over you into a blessing for you in spite of themselves. One way to please God is to dwell with your wife according to knowledge. If you don't know that she is the balance to your decision making, then it's time for you to know it now.

1Pe 3:7 Likewise, ye husbands, dwell with [them] according to knowledge, giving honour unto the wife, as unto the weaker vessel, and as being heirs together of the grace of life; **that your prayers be not hindered.**

Prayerfully create a plan together for your family, spiritually, financially and socially. Ask her what she thinks about your ideas. It's important to tell her if you are undecided so she knows what level of the process she is being included.

Here is a prayer you and your wife may want to say before you start:

> Lord Jesus forgive us of our sins, known and unknown, according to your word. Give us wisdom to make decisions that would fulfill your will for us. In Jesus' Name we pray, Amen.

I used to work for an engineering firm that often went from concept to reality. The best way to accomplish this is to have all the ideas tabled; good and bad. You would be amazed at what ideas come up if the environment allows for all ideas.

Once the ideas are written down, everyone contributes to how to accomplish each idea. Once all the ideas have been entertained, everyone votes on the best idea that can be supported most efficiently. Try this with the goals you have set with your wife. Also, like my past job, revisit your goals and decision regularly to ensure that they are still lining up. If not, you may need to ask if the goal should be changed or the decision. Again, these questions are for you and your wife to decide.

Your wife has an intuition that you must learn to trust. Using your goals as a guide, engage in a conversation with her. Sometime during the conversation, ask her how she feels about the goals and the decision that you both have made. After she shares how she feels, you might want to ask her if she still wants to go in that direction.

She is living in the process that you both are working together and deciding your future; this hits a core need that she has. Don't under estimate the power that this produces between you both.

If you guys find yourself in disagreement, I encourage you to pray and take this as a sign of bad timing. Many good ideas at the wrong time can be disastrous.

Don't let this process be the catalyst for arguments. Stay calm, allowing everyone to be honest will bring the best results. The trick is to not allow yourself to get too emotionally connected to one decision. Remember that God can bring you both into agreement. Spend your time looking for agreement. Pray about the rest. Below is another technique that my wife and I use on occasion to ensure that we are making the right decision at the right time.

ANOTHER DECISION PROCESS

My wife and I use a particular scripture to make decisions when we aren't in agreement or don't know what God wants us to do.

We pray:

> "Lord Jesus forgive us of our sins, known and unknown, according to your word. Put us at one mind and accord with your spirit."
>
> "Lord, would you have us to XXXXXX?
>
> --- we listen for an answer ---
>
> Let's say one of us heard a Yes and we agree to use that answer. Then we pray:
>
> "Spirit that would have us XXXXXX, do you confess that Jesus Christ was come in the flesh?"
>
> --- if we both hear a yes, we know it's from God. ---
>
> --- if we hear no, nothing or an answer that interrupts our question, we know it's not from God. ---
>
> ---if we get a yes and a no, then it may not be the right time to do that, so we revisit it at another time. ---

This process comes from 1John 4:1-3.

1Jo 4:1 ¶ Beloved, believe not every spirit, but try the spirits whether they are of God: because many false prophets are gone out into the world. **2** Hereby know ye the Spirit of God: **Every spirit that confesseth that Jesus Christ is come in the flesh is of God: 3** And **every spirit that confesseth**

not that Jesus Christ is come in the flesh is not of God: and this is that spirit of antichrist, whereof ye have heard that it should come; and even now already is it in the world.

Make no mistake about it. All of God's angels will politely wait for you to finish asking before they will answer. They are also bold to confess that Jesus Christ came in the flesh without hesitation. All other responses are not from God.

Tool #7

Give What You're Given

My wife's birthday was coming up and I asked my daughter and son what we should get her. My son (6 yrs.) immediately said "Let's get her a train set!" I learned an important principle here. We often give others what we want. Even as adults, we don't always investigate what someone else would like.

It is normal for two people in a marriage to have different needs. Finding out what your mate's needs are can be difficult. However, paying attention to your wife, you can learn how to meet her needs.

We humans have a habit giving to others what we desire to receive. If your wife gives you a lot of kisses, then she would love it if you would give her a lot of kisses. In fact, the more one receives what they need, the less they give what they like to receive. This is an excellent indicator on when they really have a need. If you notice that she has been touching you more often, then you can start touching her and you will meet her need.

Let me give you an example: I'm a touchy/feely person. My wife is not. I've noticed that when I want to be touched by her, I start touching her more often. This is such a subconscious act that I don't realize that I'm doing it at first. However, when she touches me, I drink it in like a cool refreshing drink after working outside in the sun. I just love it when she touches me; I can't get enough! I love it when she takes my hand, puts her arm in my arm, pats me on the rear, plays with my hair, etc...

So take the time to observe what your wife is giving you and try to give it back. If it is pleasant, good, caring and does not contradict the Word of God, it will be a good thing to return.

Some observations you may make are:

Does she do little things for you?

Is she a romantic type?

Does she touch you a lot?

Does she cook for you?

Does she listen to you?

Does she talk to you?

Does she give good massages?

These are some examples of what you can observe and then do them for her. You can even ask her about these topics; you may be surprised at her answers. Take the time to write a list of observations and then try them on her. Don't cross off anything until you ask her how she liked what you did. Her nonverbal response won't always agree with how she liked something. Get a verbal response.

Tool #8

Artificial Intuition (AI)

Women are naturally intuitive. It is one of the gifts taken from Adam that God gave a majority to Eve. It is the reason that wives are the best judge of women when it comes to their spouse. If your wife tells you that she doesn't trust a woman, you would be wise to heed to her warning. Women know women far better than we men do.

With that said, men are not as intuitive. Men, your task is to learn how to improve your artificial intuition. Listen to her and see if you can anticipate how to roll with her. They seem to like this a lot!

To give you an example, my wife likes it when I ask her if I can help her rather than having to ask. I don't always get it right but I keep trying.

Remind your wife that you don't always have your intuitive cap on and ask for a little patience. Ask her to charge your shortcomings to your head and not your heart. Additionally, tell her that you don't mind doing things for her.

When it comes to listening to your wife de-stress, you may not know when she is actually de-stressing. Men, ask your wife if she wants you to get involved or just listen when she is talking to you. This helps when you are not sure what role to play at the moment.

Tool #9

Changing Channels

This section reminds me of two types of changes: Conversations and Maturity. For some reason this makes sense to me so please indulge me on this one.

CONVERSATION

I can be in the middle of a conversation with my wife and out of nowhere; she starts on a different subject. This is not a bad thing; it's just a woman thing. I spent some time observing my wife with her sisters and they go a mile a minute while changing subjects and all of them are in lock step. No one misses a beat. It's incredible to watch. I marvel at the speed and perception at which they communicate. If I could harness that ability I would be the greatest man alive!

Normally, if my wife changes channel on me, I try to listen a little longer to see if I can get back on track. However, my wife is patient with me when I ask "Did we change channels?" She graciously catches me up and then we are off and running again.

Changing channels happens to both of you. Sometimes you changed channels while talking to your wife. Try to keep your wife updated on your perspective why you said what you said.

This is a good time to welcome yourself into the human race. We all get frustrated when we run into confusing situations. Our goal is to not allow it to take our peace.

AS WE MATURE

After being married since 1984, I've noticed that my wife and I have changed. We both have different priorities than when we were younger. Our favorite foods have changed. And many other things have changed.

This is where communication is vital for both of you. What you liked earlier in the marriage may have changed. Talk with your spouse and make the effort to honor each other's changes. Men, when informing your spouse of a change, it may be helpful for you to whisper to her.

The only consistent thing you can count on is CHANGE. So don't be thrown off by it; expect it; embrace it. Changing channels can be very rewarding and fun.

Tool #10

Types of Authority

There are three types of authority that you should be aware of: Civil Authority, Domestic Authority and Spiritual Authority. These are distinct and separate. Many times we are tempted to blend them and that can cause some frustration.

CIVIL AUTHORITY

Policemen, Judges, and civic law operate under this type of authority. Their jurisdiction is defined by the law. If we disobey the law, we can be held accountable by the enforcers of the law. It is no surprise to see a female police woman or judge who enforces the law. They are operating within their jurisdiction and it is a good thing. They are performing a leadership role. If I am pulled over by a female police officer or in the courtroom with a female judge, I have no problem submitting to their authority.

DOMESTIC AUTHORITY

In a family, God places the responsibility of the family on the man. God holds the man responsible for leading the family in a Godly manor. He is the point of contact as far as God is concerned. Like the other authorities, someone has to be placed in the leadership role. It is the nature of things that all those who are not placed in the position of authority are expected to submit. I know that this may be a sensitive subject for the ladies, however, God has not changed his mind on the issue.

Men, you may want to give your wife my book "The Wife's Secret Weapon" rather than telling her this yourself.

SPIRITUAL AUTHORITY

Spiritually, the bible relays that there is neither man nor woman in heaven. It is no surprise to see male and female spiritual leaders; to include male and female apostles, prophets, evangelists, pastors and teachers. It is possible for a male pastor to be the spiritual leader of his church and get a ticket for speeding from a female police officer.

These authorities have different jurisdictions. This is why a female pastor can be the spiritual leader of her church and come under submission to her husband when she is home.

All spiritual leaders must show a lifestyle pleasing to the Lord in all jurisdictions they find themselves in. Additionally, they must be aware of their jurisdiction.

Men, this book was written for you. I promise that "The Wife's Secret Weapon" deals with the women as well.

Tool #11

Menopause

Much has been written about menopause. Men, be aware that your wife's sexual needs may not keep up with yours. This is when you need to be as supportive and patient as possible.

Mood Swings. Some women have pre-menstrual syndrome (PMS) which causes mood swings. Your objective is not to get upset when you are confronted with them. Realize that having a board meeting to logically discuss issues will not be productive. Instead, tell her that you love her and you want the best for her. Be willing to sit with her while she expresses herself. Just don't run away. If you must go to work, tell her that you would sit with her but you have to go to work. It's O.K. to ask her "What can I do to help you feel better?".

The same technique can help you work through menopause with your wife. Chemically, her body is going through a large imbalance and she may become irritable. This is not a time to point out her shortcomings. Menopause does not mean that you must stop having sex. But you will need to communicate with your wife.

I am reminded of Sarah who was well stricken in years when God promised Abram a son in his old age. Sarah said "shall I have pleasure?"

Ge 18:1 ¶ And the LORD appeared unto Abraham in the plains of Mamre: and he sat in the tent door in the heat of the day; **2** And he lift up his eyes and looked, and, lo, three men stood by him: and when he saw [them], he ran to meet them from the tent door, and bowed himself toward the ground, **3** And said, My Lord, if now I have found favour in thy sight, pass not away, I pray thee, from thy servant: **4** Let a little water, I pray you, be fetched, and wash your feet, and rest yourselves under the tree: **5** And I will fetch a morsel of bread, and comfort ye your hearts; after that ye shall pass on: for therefore are ye come to your servant. And they said, So do, as thou hast said. **6** And Abraham hastened into the tent unto Sarah, and said, Make ready quickly three measures of fine meal, knead [it], and make cakes upon the hearth. **7** And Abraham ran unto the herd, and fetcht a calf tender and good, and gave [it] unto a young man; and he hasted to dress it. **8** And he took butter, and milk, and the calf which he had dressed, and set [it] before them; and he stood by them under the tree, and they did eat. **9** ¶ And they said unto him, Where [is] Sarah thy wife? And he said, Behold, in the tent. **10** And he said, I will certainly return unto thee according to the time of life; and, lo, Sarah thy wife shall have a son. And Sarah heard [it] in the tent door, which [was] behind him. **11** Now Abraham and Sarah [were] old [and] well stricken in age; [and] it ceased to be with Sarah after the manner of women. **12** Therefore Sarah laughed within herself, saying, After I am waxed old shall I have pleasure, my lord being old also?

Notice that the relationship with God transcended past their age limitation? Let your relationship with Jesus transcend any obstacles you may have. God works in and through us on this three-dimensional world both spiritually and naturally.

The purpose of this section is to help you mitigate the obstacles introduced when menopause arrives. For some women, menopause causes the uterus to produce less lubricant during sex; this can be the reason for more discomfort or pain while having sex.

I encourage you to speak with your doctor about sex being less enjoyable or even painful. They will be able to give you the best advice for your particular situation.

Some conversations with our doctor and friends of similar age have mentioned the following:

> One of our doctors have said that more sex helps reduce the discomfort.

> A friend mentioned olive oil for her and her husband has helped significantly.

> The internet has revealed several natural products that have very positive reviews.

Men, be willing to help your wife figure out what works best for her to enjoy sex. Please pray that God restore her, just as He restored Sarah. Most of all, have fun.

Tool #12

Timing is Everything!

Even in ministry, a couple can be so busy that they cannot spend the time required to talk about important issues. This is very dangerous as it creates a lot of collateral damage.

My wife and I are very busy in the morning getting ready for work or church. If we have not had enough time to discuss important issues throughout the week, it will begin to surface while trying to get ready in the morning. This is a recipe for a bad morning. Our comments are quick and rushed and there is no guarantee that I (a non-verbally stimulated man) will say what I really mean. This will lead to misunderstanding and offense. Additionally, it will take more time of the morning to clear up and possibly cause one or both of us to be late. For us, the mornings are not a good time for us to discuss serious issues.

Find out a good time to talk about serious and lengthy matters that allows you both to have time to respond thoughtfully and unrushed.

Some pastors take every Monday off to dedicate it to their family. I love that. It reminds us all that Christianity must include success in the family. My real point here is that you must set aside some time with your spouse alone to talk about small things, middle things and big things.

We men are sometimes afraid to talk because we don't want to say anything to offend our spouse or cause a division. Our defensiveness will cause us to either say nothing or speak harshly. This is where the challenges help her become less defensive.

Men, if you practice expressing yourself to your wife, you will get better and it will get easier.

Tool #13

Boundaries; Your Protection!

Where ever you go in life, opportunities to take things to extreme are always available. Boundaries are a way to prepare and protect yourself from unexpected surprises that would normally catch you off guard.

Because we are talking in reference to relationships, I want to focus on some good ground rules that help you set up great boundaries to protect you from yourself, the world and the enemy.

1. Don't allow yourself to think that you can handle it without boundaries; pride comes before a fall.

   > **Pr 16:18** ¶ Pride [goeth] before destruction, and an haughty spirit before a fall.

2. Never do/say anything with/to the opposite sex that you would not do/say in front of your spouse. (If you are not married, then consider Jesus as your spouse.)
3. Put yourself in your spouse's place. How would you want your spouse to honor the relationship?
4. Share your boundaries with your spouse. Create an open forum to allow for modifications to be made so that both parties are respecting each other to the level required. DO NOT fall prey to the mindset "Common sense would tell you that...". Assume nothing and

don't expect the other person to be a mind reader on your expectations.

5. Pornography must be avoided at all costs! Some say you can look but you cannot touch. Jesus says:

Mt 5:27 ¶ Ye have heard that it was said by them of old time, Thou shalt not commit adultery: **28** But I say unto you, That whosoever looketh on a woman to lust after her hath committed adultery with her already in his heart.

This principle applies to women as well.

You may need to formulate additional boundaries to enable you to live a successful Christian life.

Remember to allow your Boundary List to be a living document. In other words, revisit it and make additions and subtractions as you see necessary. It is impossible for you to create such a list and account for all that you will be confronted with. Let good counsel and experience forge your boundaries.

Jesus gave us some boundaries:

Mt 5:43 ¶ Ye have heard that it hath been said, Thou shalt love thy neighbour, and hate thine enemy. **44** But I say unto you, Love your enemies, bless them that curse you, do good to them that hate you, and pray for them which despitefully use you, and persecute you;

Mt 22:37 Jesus said unto him, Thou shalt love the Lord thy God with all thy heart, and with all thy soul, and with all thy mind. **38** This is the first and great commandment. **39** And the second [is] like unto it, Thou shalt love thy neighbour as thyself. **40** On these two commandments hang all the law and the prophets.

If you are curious what law is referenced above, here it is; the ten commandments:

Exodus 20:1 ¶ And God spake all these words, saying, **2** I am the LORD thy God, which have brought thee out of the land of Egypt, out of the house of bondage. **3** Thou shalt have no other gods before me. **4** Thou shalt not make unto thee any graven image, or any likeness of any thing that is in heaven above, or that is in the earth beneath, or that is in the water under the earth: **5** Thou shalt not bow down thyself to them, nor serve them: for I the LORD thy God am a jealous God, visiting the iniquity of the fathers upon the children unto the third and fourth generation of them that hate me; **6** And shewing mercy unto thousands of them that love me, and keep my commandments. **7** Thou shalt not take the name of the LORD thy God in vain; for the LORD will not hold him guiltless that taketh his name in vain. **8** Remember the sabbath day, to keep it holy. **9** Six days shalt thou labour, and do all thy work: **10** But the seventh day is the sabbath of the LORD thy God: in it thou shalt not do any work, thou, nor thy son, nor thy daughter, thy manservant, nor thy maidservant, nor thy cattle, nor thy stranger that is within thy gates: **11** For in six days the LORD made heaven and earth, the sea, and all that in them is, and rested the seventh day: wherefore the LORD blessed the sabbath day, and hallowed it. **12** ¶ Honour thy father and thy mother: that thy days may be long upon the land which the LORD thy God giveth thee. **13** Thou shalt not kill. **14** Thou shalt not commit adultery. **15** Thou shalt not steal. **16** Thou shalt not bear false witness against thy neighbour. **17** Thou shalt not covet thy neighbour's house, thou shalt not covet thy neighbour's wife, nor his manservant, nor his maidservant, nor his ox, nor his ass, nor any thing that is thy neighbour's.

Tool #14

Having Fun!

This is the most important dynamic in marriage. FUN! You must have some fun! So, I decided to give you some ideas. Most of these games work great for kids too. You may consider these games too immature for you. Please remember that innocent fun is the richest. It strips away the complexity and allows you to just have fun.

GAME #1

The Laughing Game

Rules:

- The goal is to make the other person laugh for real
- The last fake laugher wins the game
- See who has the best fake laugh (Snorting is allowed)
- Funny faces with the laugh are allowed
- You cannot touch the opponent (but you can get real close)
- Talk about how smart the other person was for trying a particular face and/or laugh.

GAME #2

The Noise Game

Rules:

- The goal is to convince the other person to make the noise you are making.
- You can make a train, plane, automobile, motorcycle, gun, machine gun noise. (or animal noises)
- Even if you are terrible, you must insist that it's better than theirs.
- You get a point if you get them to make the noise.
- You get a point if they agree that yours is better.
- You get a point if they take the challenge and do a different noise.

GAME #3

The Pitch Game

Rules:

- The goal is to make your opponent laugh by changing the pitch of your voice
- Say something in a higher or lower tone than usual.
- Make it as awkward sounding as possible. If it doesn't fit, you are probably on to something!
- Challenge the other person to try it.

A friend recommended a helium balloon.

GAME #?

Try to make up your own games that you both like to play. The previous games are just to get you started.

Playing card games, board games and the such is good if you both enjoy them.

While you are doing the challenges, you might want to try the first two games to keep her guessing. She may think that you have lost your mind but you will have a great time watching her not know what to make of it. On that note, if she doesn't join you, do it anyway and watch how much fun you have watching her response. Trust me when I tell you that you are getting to her!!!

12

WHAT ABOUT THE CHILDREN?

Sometimes we men need some help in relating to children. I hope that these suggestions will help you craft a technique that will best suit your situation.

As the head of the household, you have a very powerful influence on your children. Understand that it is your responsibility to speak into their lives successful things. Your praise should be lavish and more often than you correct. Take an inventory of how often you praise versus correct. Fix it.

In a world that will try to chew your children up and spit them out, you need to teach them how to be balanced in being tough and gentle. Teach them how to know when to be gentle and when to be tough. You hold their self-esteem in your hand. Be the one who points out the positive often. It is OK to tell them that you want them to do greater things than you have done; Jesus said that to us. Let them know that they will be great in the spiritual things of God, the emotional things and financial things.

Daughters – Hug them daily and let them know that you love them and are very proud of them. Let them know that you don't want anything to happen to them and that all you want to do is protect them from people who would try to harm them. They are expressers...so...

Sons – Hug them daily and let them know that you love them and are very proud of them. Let them know that you want to teach them how to be a real man and how to treat women.

Talk with your wife on the best way to encourage them in the:

Things of God.

Things of the heart.

Things of their thought life.

Things of their talents and abilities.

Things of their bright future.

You can talk about these things over dinner to your children.

THE POINT SYSTEM

Men, the way I see it, it's all a point system. You take advantage of all the opportunities to gain points.

For example, you get a can of shaving cream and set it down in front of the children or child. Say Go! Grab the can, fill the shirt and splat the shirt!!! POINTS!

> **NOTE:** Don't use menthol shaving cream because it burns.... Just sayin.

Water balloon fights.... POINTS!

Throwing the kids in the pool... POINTS!

Throwing the kids down the snow bank... POINTS!

SO, when your child has a degree in criminal justice and she can beat you in an argument, you can reply... You'll never catch me, I've got too many points!

FINALLY, AND MOST IMPORTANTLY!

Talking to your children about your spouse in a negative light will backfire on you in a BIG way. No matter what side they take, they will resent you for making them choose. This also applies to parents who are no longer in the picture or are separated. Children, if encouraged to respect their other parents will honor you and still decide for themselves about the other. If you know the other parent is not good for the child, you will do well enforcing them to send birthday cards and respect that parent. THEY WILL DECIDE. Just don't be collateral damage because you tried to tell them the truth.

Another way to destroy your credibility with them is if you use them to get even with the other parent. Children are more perceptive than you think. If they feel that for some reason you are denying them access to the other parent, they will begin to distance themselves from you. If the other parent will not hurt the child, you should never be the reason they cannot spend time together.

13

IRON SHARPENS IRON

CONFLICT AT ITS BEST

OK! You know about your tool box and hopefully you have used it to find that it gives you positive results. But maybe you slipped and went back into your old mode of operation. No problem! Just get back up and use your tool box.

The bible reads:

Proverbs 24:16 For a just [man] falleth seven times, and riseth up again: but the wicked shall fall into mischief.

You qualify to be just when you get back up! The falling is for everyone, getting back up is for the just!

THE PURPOSE OF CONFLICT

In a marriage, God uses conflict for his purposes. Not to tear you down but to smooth out some rough edges in your life. I know that you think that you are all that and a bag of chips. I definitely encourage that type of confidence. However, God wants to take you higher. The bible also reads:

Proverbs 27:17 ¶ Iron sharpeneth iron; so a man sharpeneth the countenance of his friend.

One of the ways that you know that you are smoothing a metal surface is that sparks fly. The goal here is to learn to use your tool box when you feel those sparks flying.

YOUR COUNTENANCE

Not always are we aware of what our countenance looks like; you need your spouse to help you with that. This begs the question "What does countenance mean?"

Countenance in Hebrew is פנים paniym (pronounced paw-neem') meaning presence, sight, face.

Its root word is פנה panah (pronounced paw-naw') meaning to turn toward, to turn from, look, prepare, regard, and respect. Keep your countenance towards God and turn away from ungodly things. Your goal here is to resort to your tool box when you are upset as well as when you are not.

Regardless of the situation, you don't need to let your countenance drop.

EVERYTHING DOES NOT NEED TO BE FIXED!

Out of our protective nature, we have a proclivity to fix things. Sometimes we have to accept the idea that a particular subject or argument is a dead end. Stop going there; let it lie. We don't need everything to be fixed right now. How do you know if something is a dead end? I will answer this by my testimony.

MY TESTAMONY

My nature is to fix everything. I am a problem solver; very analytical. In the past, I would speak my mind without invitation (this is not a Godly trait) and try to make her see my point. One night my wife and I had a spat at bed time. She was so irritated with me that she went and slept in our guest room. The next morning, I held my peace and just acted like nothing happened. She acted a little differently but I acted like everything was fine. If she needed to address the issue, she could bring it up; I was not going to. This allowed us to continue with having a nice day together.

On most occasions, this approach causes issues to dissipate quickly and things are so much easier now. Resolving all arguments is unnecessary.

I know that you might be saying that this is hard. I just want to remind you that the art of learning another skill is repetition. Remember!

Phillipians 4:13 I can do all things through Christ which strengtheneth me.

14

TAKE ACTION

It's time to take action! Make sure that you have fun too.

I want to give you some action items for you to accomplish. Don't let more than four days go by without doing one of these items. If you are going for shock and awe, do one every other day. You may not be able to do these in order, the point is that you try to find a way to accomplish them all.

YOUR CHALLENGES!

1. Tell her that you love her every day, she will never get tired of hearing it.
2. Hold her without touching her sexually.
3. Wash her feet.

> Get a pan, a couple of drops of olive oil, message the oil into her feet, take your time, speak good things to her and tell her all the things that you appreciate about her. End with telling her that she is your queen.

4. Bathe your wife.

Shower with your wife, bathe her, do not initiate sex for that night. If your wife initiates sex, then become her servant and ask her how you may serve her; this is all about her.

5. Ask her if there is anything you can do for her.
6. Do the dishes.
7. Take the kids while she gets a break.
8. Clean the house; maybe one room at a time.
9. Do the laundry.
10. Clean her car.
11. Text her that you are thinking of her fondly.
12. Call her during the day to say hello.
13. Have a lunch date.
14. Buy her flowers
15. Buy her an "I love you" card unexpectedly.
16. Take her to get a pedicure/manicure.
17. Take her to a Hotel for one night or weekend.
18. Play a game with her.

REFERENCES

Hebrew and Chaldee Lexicon to the Old Testament, Gesenius and Fürst, Boston: A.I. Bradley & Co.

James Strong, Abingdon's Strong's Exhaustive Concordance of the Bible, New Jersey, 1890 – James Strong, Key Word Comparison 1980 – Abingdon

Software: *Online Bible Edition*, Authorized Version of the King James Bible, Strong's Concordance
Version 2.00.04, June 2006

Thompson Chain Reference Study Bible King James Version, Kirkbride Bible Company, Inc. Indiana, 1988

Works by Pastor Steve Morgan

~ First Things First (What Every Christian Should Know)

Christianity is really very easy. This book shows you how scriptures make it so easy. If you are a new believer or a believer who is returning to your first love, this is for you. First Things First starts from receiving Christ into your heart and finishes with some basic principles to build on a foundation laid by the word of God. Pastor Steve also shares some personal testimonies with the principles learned that will help you avoid some of the challenges he faced as a new born again believer.

~ Second Things Second (The Doctrine of Christ)

This book covers the principles of the doctrine of Christ as mentioned in Hebrews 6:1~2. We will cover the six pillars mentioned here.

To be perfect you must stay under the grace of God. To do that you must learn more of His provisions for you. These can be found in the Doctrine of Christ. The foundation of the Doctrine of Christ is supported by six pillars which are:

- Repentance From Dead Works
- Faith Toward God
- The Doctrine Of Baptisms
- Laying On Of Hands
- Resurrection Of The Dead

- Eternal Judgment

Every Christian should be encouraged by Hebrews 6:1~2 to learn of these pillars and build a foundation that cannot be moved.

~ God's Blueprint for Spiritual Growth and Reward
(The Mosaic Tabernacle)

There are many examples of how we are to grow in God's likeness. The Tabernacle, built under the supervision of Moses, is also a map to maturity. Here you will learn some of the depths of God and His commitment to maintaining a relationship with you.

~ The Wife's Secret Weapon

Relationships are very easy but they require special tools you already have. With this book, you will learn about your "Secret Weapon". This "Secret Weapon will empower you to reach your husband emotionally deeper than ever before. You will learn how to get past the WALL that seems to frustrate you when you speak to your spouse. He will actually respond to you like a real human being! Can you imagine him talking to you in more than a few words at a time? This book will show you how to draw this person out. He really is your perfect man! When you have accomplished all the challenges in this book, you will have increased in influence in the marriage by 100 fold. This is the latest information on communicating across gender lines. If you wish that you could get your point across to the opposite sex, this book gives you what you need to succeed while having fun doing it. You won't believe how powerful these tools are until you try them!

~ The Husband's Toolbox

Relationships are really very easy, but they require special tools you already have. With this book, you will learn how to use them to their full benefit. You will also discover why your wife is the way she is and how to work with her as you were designed by God! You will learn how to make sure she never wants to leave your side. After completing the challenges in this book, you will have obtained your rightful position as the Man of your house. This is the latest information on communicating across gender lines. If you wish that you could get your point across to the opposite sex, this book gives you what you need to succeed! You won't believe how powerful these tools are until you try them!

PASTOR STEVE MORGAN's CREDENTIALS

Alumni of Sonship School of the Firstborn
    Bishop Nathaniel Holcomb
    Covenant Connections International (CCI)
    Kaleen, TX

Masters in Business Administration (MBA)
    Troy University
    Troy, AL

Bachelor of Arts in Business Management
    Ashford University
    Clinton, IA

Associates in Applied Science in Human Relations
    Community College of the Air Force (CCAF)

Associates in Applied Science in Electronic
Engineering Technology
    CCAF

Pastor Steve is the founder and president of For Him Ministries. He has performed as a stand-in pastor for several churches in Germany and in Florida; allowing for vacations and smooth transitions respectively. He has been used as a consultant for churches in all auxiliaries to further the work of Christ. Pastor Steve has preached all over the globe to include: Afghanistan, Africa, Czechoslovakia, Honduras, Germany, Pakistan and the United States.

Pastor Steve also served 33 years combined in the US Air Force active duty and reserves.

He can be contacted by email at:
CustomerCare@ForHimMinistries.net
www.ForHimMinistries.net

www.ingramcontent.com/pod-product-compliance
Lightning Source LLC
Chambersburg PA
CBHW060941040426
42445CB00011B/958